MICROSOFT WORD

The Ultimate Guide to Master Word Features & Commands. Become a Pro from Scratch in Just 7 Days with Step-By-Step Instructions, Clear Illustrations, and Practical Examples

Scott Burnett

ISBN: 979-8848088045
10 9 8 7 6 5 4 3 2 1

Table of Contents

Introduction

MS word 365 is the current version of MS Word. It is the new and advanced version of the word processor. It comes with various desirable features, which makes its release worthwhile and meaningful.

Word 365 comes with a 3D image compared with the previous version released before WORD 365 release, which is words 2013 and 2016. The mindset of the user is that word is only for processing word documents alone, but word 365 has changed that orientation with 3D images and graphic insertion. It is not just about inserting graphics and images; you will as well design it just as if you are using the graphic application. You can put the image into the shape to fill the shape, and you can as well insert text to the shape filled with the image and even set the alignment and direction of the text within the shape.

Aside from 3D images, there is an application called language translator, which was not available in the previous version. Word 365 settle and eliminate communication and language barrier with the app's translation which permits you to type any word, phrase, or sentence into another language. How to use a language translator with no stress has been fully explained in this user guide.

In addition to the word 365 feature, which is a side-to-side view. You can view two pages of the same document on a page by splitting the screen into two. Part of the different word 365 brings is the compound equation. You can select those equations and substitute them with the number and thereby break down every hurdle of the mathematics equation.

Furthermore, this user guide gives a summary of the various elements of the MS word 365 screens, including the backstage view option, adding page numbers to MS word documents, discovering and amending spelling mistakes, adding and customizing Headers and Footers, discovering and correcting grammar mistakes and lastly how to add ruler within the MS word.

MS word 365 offers you new and better ways of working with documents, such as side-by-side navigation, translator, and more new features. To overcome no obstacle that some call complicated obstacle, kindly pick up this user guide.

Chapter 1: **Starting Word**

Launching is a way of starting a program or an application. There are various ways of launching the Microsoft Word application, but we will be checking the two mostly used ways, which are explained in the subsequent section.

Starting Word With The Start Menu

To start Microsoft Word with the start menu, kindly:

- Click on the **window start menu** located at the bottom left or center of the desktop window.
- Scroll down to search for **Word**, then tap on it as soon as you see it. (It may be captioned as a word or word 365 depending on the version you are using).

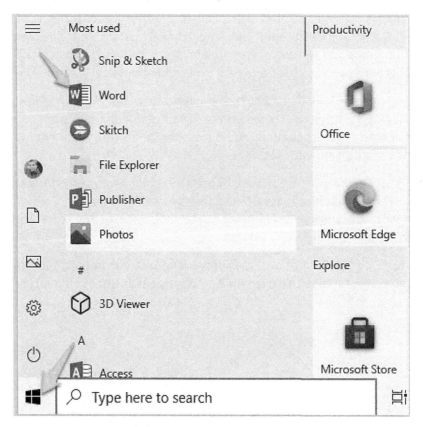

Starting Word from The Taskbar (The Fastest Means)

This is the fastest and even the easiest means of starting Microsoft Word. To make use of this method, you have to pin Microsoft Word to the taskbar first; once it is pinned to the taskbar, you will only need to single-click it on the taskbar for subsequent launching. To pin Microsoft Word to the taskbar, kindly:

- Click on the **start menu** and locate the program
- Right-click on it and select **More** from the drop-down list, then pick **"Pin to taskbar"** from the more drop-down list. Immediately the concerned program will be pinned to the taskbar.

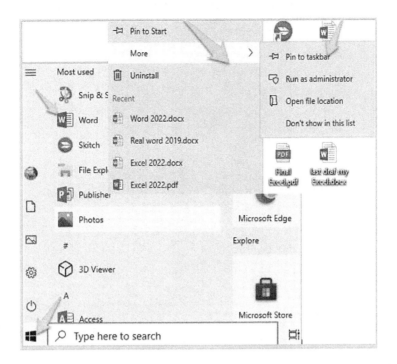

- Whenever you want to launch into the program, simply **single-click on its icon** on the taskbar.

Create A New Document

A document can be created either from the blank document or from the various available template that is available on MS word. After you are done creating the document, you can store such a document on your PC. To create the document from a blank document after you have launched into the program, kindly:

- Tap on the **blank document**, provided you have not been using the program before.

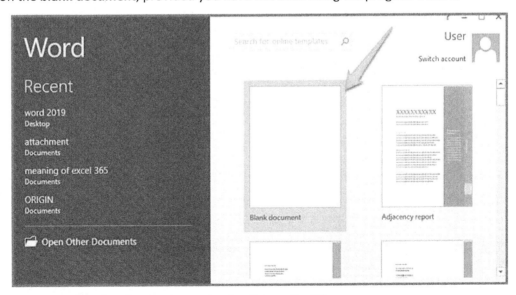

- If you are currently using the program, simply click on the **File menu**.
- Then tap on **New** from the file backstage**.**

Alternatively: after you have opened the Word main screen, press **Ctrl + N** on the keyboard for new document shortcuts.

To start from the template, simply click on **any template** of your choice from the available template, and it will be opened up.

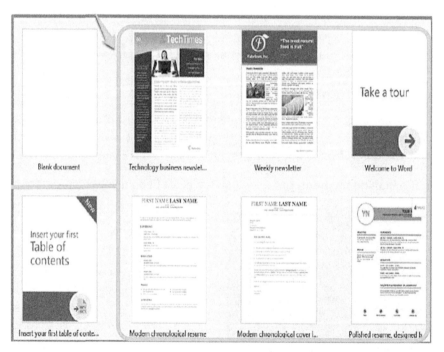

Observing The Microsoft Word Start Screen

Immediately after you launch word 2022, the first screen you will notice is known as the start screen. You can perform various activities with the start screen, as listed below:

- Select a document from the group of the **previous document** you have accessed in a recent time.
- Search for **any other document** inside your Word document.
- Click on the **Blank document** to create a new document.
- **Featured** is used to show various word online templates.
- **Personal** is a link to show each of the templates you customize by yourself.
- Type your desired template into **the search box** to run a check for you on the available template, e.g. (birthday format or Easter party).

- Select a template from available **offline templates.**

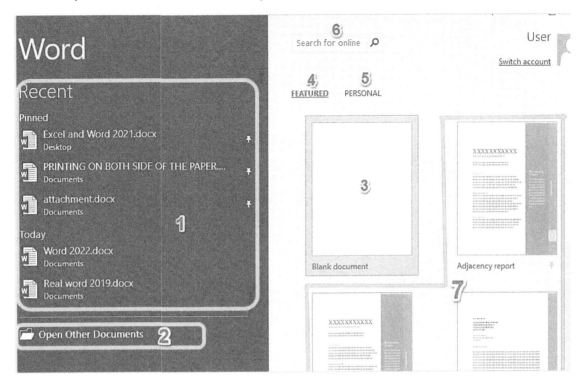

Observing MS Word Main Screen

The main screen shows the principal components of the word 2022 interface. Let us delve into those components:

- **The title bar:** the title bar will show the name you use to save your document. The default name is document 1 if you have not used any name to save your document at all.
- **Quick Access toolbar:** it contains a quick element that you can use to extract commands out of the available toolbar, such as On/Off, save, undo, redo, etc.
- **Tab:** a particular title or name given to each group of the ribbon.
- **Ribbon**: it shows a group of connected commands under each tab.
- **Command group:** this represents the gallery of related tools within tabs. For instance, within the Home tab, there are multiple commands such as Clipboard, Editing, Fonts, Paragraph, and so on.
- **Horizontal Ruler:** it is mainly used for measuring working areas horizontally.
- **Vertical Ruler**: it is used for measuring the working area vertically.
- **Cursor pointer:** it is where your typing entry will start from.
- **Scroll bar:** it is used to scroll up, down, left, or right within the given document.
- **Working area:** this is the largest area on the main screen. It is the area that will accommodate all your text entries.
- **Status bar**: it gives an exact description of your documents, such as the number of pages and words.
- **The view option**: the view option shows the current view option, such as Read mode, Print layout, and web layout.
- **Zoom slider:** it is used to adjust (increase or reduce) the size of the window screen.

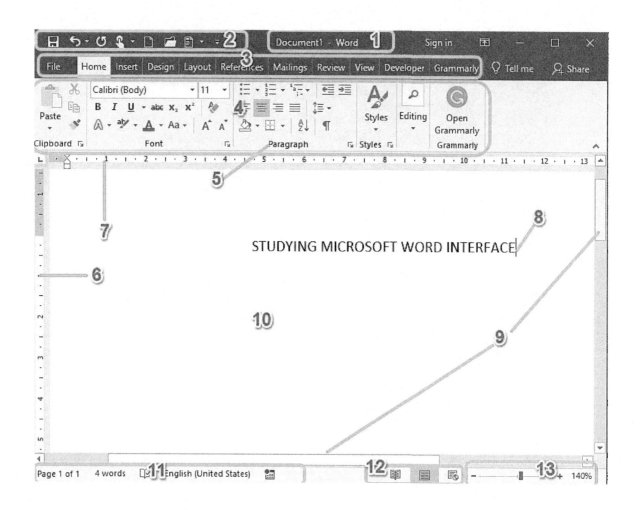

STUDYING MICROSOFT WORD INTERFACE

Chapter 2: **The Main Screen**

The Home Ribbon

In MS Word, the "Home" tab is the one that comes up when you open the program. It's usually broken down into groups: the Clipboard, Font, Style, and Editing. It lets you choose the color, font, emphasis, bullets, and where your text is. Besides that, there are also options to cut, copy, and paste in it. After selecting the home tab, you will get more options to work with.

The Insert Ribbon

This part can be used to input anything into your document. Examples of things you can insert are tables, words, shapes, hyperlinks, charts, signature lines, time, shapes, headers, footers, text boxes, links, boxes, equations, and so on.

The Design Ribbon

Here, you can choose from documents with centered titles, off-centered headings, left-justified text, and more. You can also choose from a variety of page borders, watermarks, and colors in the design tab.

The Page Layout Ribbon

You can use it to make your Microsoft Word documents look the way you want them to look. It has options to set margins, show line numbers, set paragraph indentation, apply themes, control page orientation and size, line breaks, and more.

The References Ribbon

This tab allows you to add references to a document and then make a bibliography at the end of the text so you can look back at it. It's common for the references to be stored in a master list, which is used to add references to other documents. It has options like a table of contents, footnotes, citations and bibliography, captions, index, table of authorities, smart look, etc.

The Review Ribbon

The Review Tab has commenting, language, translation, spell check, word count, and other tools for you to use. A good thing about it is that you can find and change comments very quickly. These options will display when you click on the review tab.

The Mailings Ribbon

One of the best things about Microsoft Word is that you can write a letter, report, etc. and send it to a lot of people at the same time, with each person's name and address in the letter.

The View Ribbon

In the View tab, you can switch between a single page and a double page. You can also change how the layout tools work. You can use it to make a print layout, outline, website, task pane, toolbar, and rulers, as well as to make a full-screen view, zoom in and out, and so on.

Fil Backstage

The "File" menu tab contains the menu options related to document file management. This is occasionally referred to as the backstage perspective. The "File" menu tab provides the menu options required for document editing. It's called backstage since it's not utilized for text entry or editing. It includes document status information and menu choices for viewing, printing, saving, and safeguarding the document. Additionally, it has configuration options.

You'll note that the "File" option is unique among Word's tabs. By selecting the "File" menu tab, the current document is completely replaced with the "File" menu items. By clicking on another tab, a new set of icons in the ribbon area becomes available for usage with the currently open document.

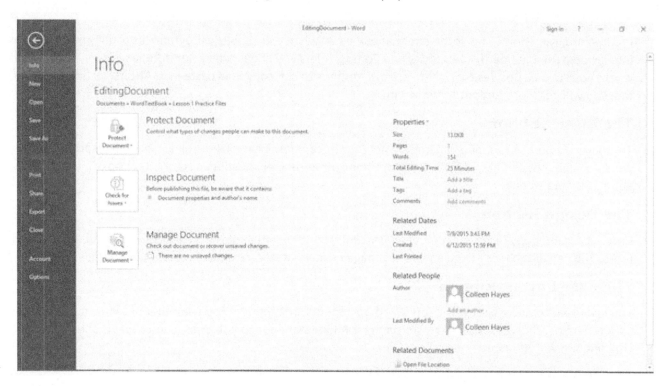

The left column of the "File" menu comprises key categories of document-related actions. The "Info" section of the "File" menu provides information about the current document and its contributors.

The "New" submenu of the "File" menu has options for generating new documents. This is the same view that was presented when Word was opened for the first time. You'll note that you have the option of creating a blank document or one that is based on a template. Templates are advantageous because they frequently contain data, formatting, and computations associated with popular word processing documents such as reports, letters, resumes, and flyers.

The "Open" option is used to provide a separate document for Word to open. You can open recently used documents or pick a document stored on OneDrive (a Microsoft cloud service) or locally on your computer.

Typically, you'll open files with the.doc or.docx extension. The.doc extension refers to documents stored in Microsoft Word 2007 or older versions. The.docx files are those saved in the Microsoft Word 2010/2013/2016/2019 format. Word is backward compatible, meaning it can open and edit both types of files.

Additionally, Word has a handy feature that will open.pdf files and convert them to the editable Word format. This converting ability is advantageous if you need to modify a pdf file. Occasionally, not all of the pdf file's contents, notably the picture layout and formatting, are converted successfully. As we shall see later, Word can also save documents in the pdf format.

The "Save" and "Save As" menu choices enable you to (1) save the current document, (2) save a copy of it with a different name or location, or (3) save a copy of it as a different file type. These settings may be advantageous as you acquire familiarity with some of Word's more complex functions. The illustration depicts a variety of various file formats that can be used to save your content. Take note that one of the save-as options includes a pdf version.

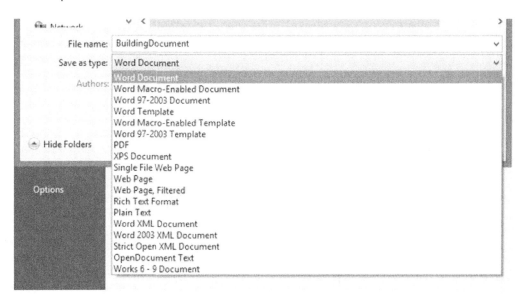

The "Print" menu section includes options for printing a document. These things include selecting the appropriate printer, controlling the printer's different features, and printing a document. Additionally, the "Print" tab gives a sample of how a document will appear when printed.

The "Share" menu option provides productivity tools that make it simple to share your work with coworkers. You should click on the other navigation items to access the submenu items' choices. The "Share" option is frequently advantageous when working in a team endeavor. The same outcomes may be obtained outside of word by sending email attachments or uploading your work to the cloud. However, the facilities included in Microsoft Word make it simple to share your work. The four submenu items are as follows:

- Share with Others—save to the cloud and send a link to a colleague.
- Send the document through email as a.doc or.pdf attachment, or share a link to a previously saved document.
- Present Online—upload it to a website where it may be seen using a browser.

- Post to Blog—publish it to your blog.

The "Export" tab enables you to convert your work to a different file type (such as.pdf) for evaluation by colleagues who prefer to use a different program. This option duplicates some of the functionality of the "Save As" file type.

The "Close" menu item effectively closes the currently open document. The "Options" menu item group enables you to adjust Word's design and functionality. Finally, you may manage your Microsoft accounts using the "Account" menu.

Chapter 3: **Editing on Microsoft Word**

Applying Styles to Text and Paragraphs

- Highlight the text to be altered

  ### Word's for Printing

  A Word document is formatted to fit on a specific size page with the text automatically flowing from one page to the next. Excel supports printing, but its page breaks are not obvious, and because it's printing area can extend multiple pages horizontally as well as vertically the page breaks can be difficult to manage.

- Go to the "Home tab," which is your default displayed Word 365 interface

- On your right-hand side, second to the last, you will see the "Styles" ribbon

- Select one of the styles above; you can also click on the drop-down arrow to view other styles. Let's

  assume we choose "Heading 1"

Word's for Printing

A Word document is formatted to fit on a specific size page with the text automatically flowing from one page to the next. Excel supports printing, but its page breaks are not obvious, and because it's printing area can extend multiple pages horizontally as well as vertically the page breaks can be difficult to manage.

- Your highlighted text will be converted to the selected style, which is "Heading 1"
- You can also do something similar to your paragraph by also highlighting it

  ### Word's for Printing

  A Word document is formatted to fit on a specific size page with the text automatically flowing from one page to the next. Excel supports printing, but its page breaks are not obvious, and because it's printing area can extend multiple pages horizontally as well as vertically the page breaks can be difficult to manage.

- Go to the "Home tab," which is your default displayed Word 365 screen

- On your right-hand side, locate the "Style" ribbon

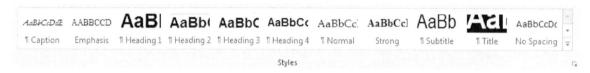

- Now, let's select the second heading, which is "Heading 2"

Word's for Printing

A Word document is formatted to fit on a specific size page with the text automatically flowing from one page to the next. Excel supports printing, but its page breaks are not obvious, and because it's printing area can extend multiple pages horizontally as well as vertically the page breaks can be difficult to manage.

- Your paragraph text will change to "Heading 2" styling

Creating a New Style

- Go to the "Home tab"

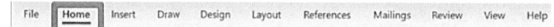

On your right-hand side, second to the last ribbon, you will see "Styles," select the dropdown arrow as illustrated below

You will be shown different options; among the options, choose "Create a Style"

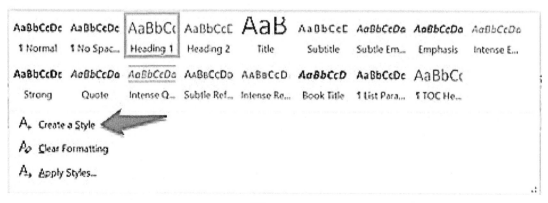

- Another dialog box will pop-up titled "Name," name it according to your choice

- Then, select "Modify" for more modifications to your newly created style

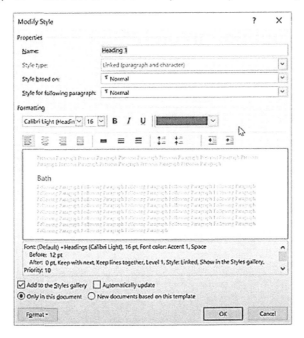

Once done, click "Ok," your newly created style will be added to the styles list

Renaming Styles

- Make sure your text that carries a style format is highlighted to recognize the specific style to be renamed

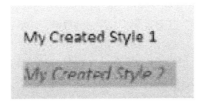

- Go to the "Home tab"

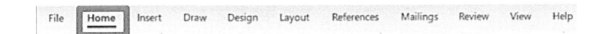

- On your right-hand side, you will see the "styles" ribbon

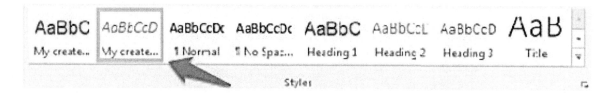

- Below the "styles" ribbon, click on the little arrow

- A dialog box will appear, indicating your selected or created style

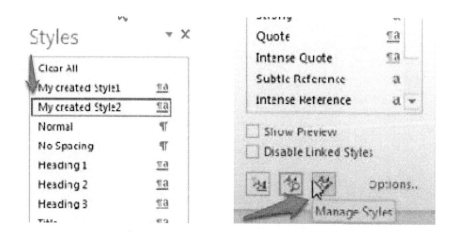

- Below the "Styles displayed box," select the last option "Manage Styles." Double-click on "Manage Styles"

- Another dialog box will appear; make sure your style is highlighted as indicated in the illustration below, then click on "Modify"

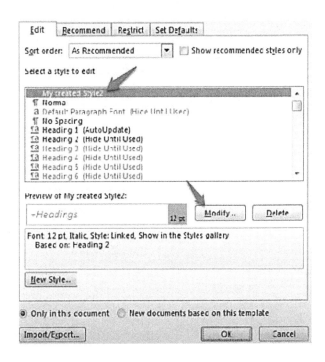

- You will be brought to the modification box named "Properties." This is where your selected style can be edited, renamed, and your font size, style, color, alignment, and the rest can be worked upon. Once done, hit "ok"

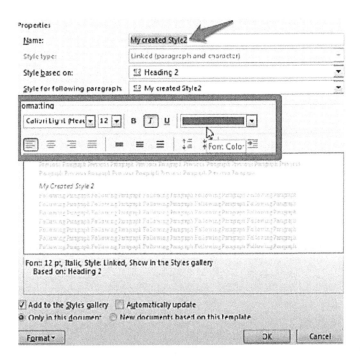

- Let's assume I renamed my style from "My created Style 2" to "My 2"

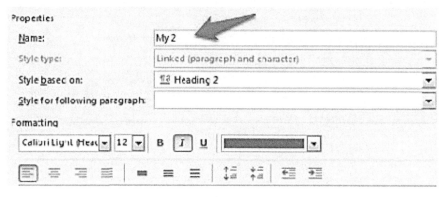

Once done, click "ok"

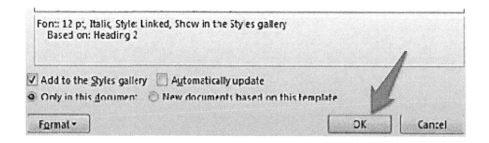

- Your previous displayed box titled "Manage styles" will also affect the new changes; click "ok" to see your styles ribbon having the same effect

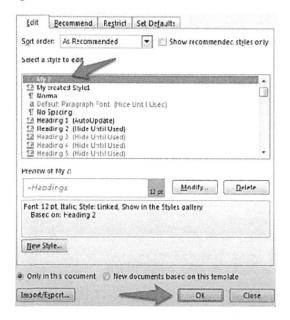

- Now, you will see the changes we made on renaming our style from "My created Style 2" to "My 2"

Editing Paragraph Styles

Modification is majorly in two ways: you either modify your existing style or your created style. I explained *"Creating a New Style"* and illustrated how to change it. Here, I will be demonstrating how to modify existing styles

- Go to the "Home tab"

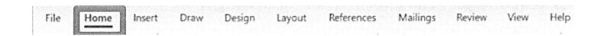

- On your right-hand side, you will see the "Styles" ribbon. Assuming we want to modify "Heading 1", right-click on it, and a dialog box will appear with many options, select "Modify"

- Here is where your "Heading 1" modification which is one of the existing styles on your list. You can modify the font style, font size, boldness, color, and many more. For simplicity and illustration purpose, click on "color" and choose "red" color, then click "Ok."

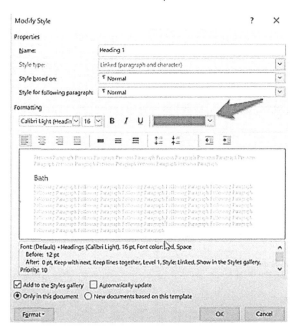

- Note the changes, "Heading 1," which is one of the existing styles, will have the effect of the color red, which we modified to

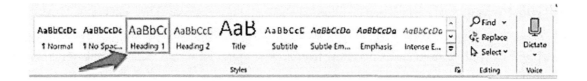

Bold, Italic & Underlined

To Bold Text & Adjust The Font Size By Increasing It

To bold text, select the portion you want to bold, then go to the home tab and select the **B** icon, which stands for bold. Your text will be in bold format; make sure it is still highlighted, then also go to font size as indicated below through the pink arrow, click on it or type the font size you want. You can use **Ctrl + B** as a shortcut to bold text.

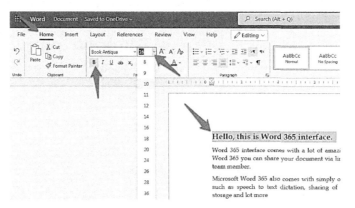

Underlining Your Text

Go to the home tab

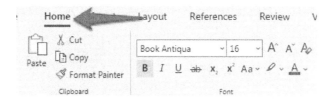

Make sure the text you want to underline is highlighted

Hello, this is Word 365 interface.

Word 365 interface comes with a lot of amazing features for Microsoft users with Word 365 you can share your document via link and track your progress with your team member.

Microsoft Word 365 also comes with simply outlook for user friendly environment such as speech to text dictation, sharing of document via link, OneDrive cloud storage and lot more

Select the underlined icon (U)

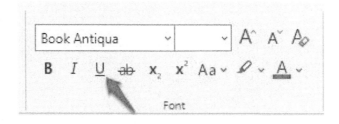

Your highlighted text will become underlined

Hello, this is Word 365 interface.

Word 365 interface comes with a lot of amazing features for Microsoft users with Word 365 you can share your document via link and track your progress with your team member.

Microsoft Word 365 also comes with simply outlook for user friendly environment such as speech to text dictation, sharing of document via link, OneDrive cloud storage and lot more

Italicizing Your Text

Go to the "home tab" and select the text to be italicized by highlighting it with your mouse

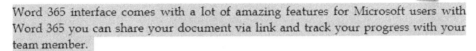

Hello, this is Word 365 interface.

Word 365 interface comes with a lot of amazing features for Microsoft users with Word 365 you can share your document via link and track your progress with your team member.

Microsoft Word 365 also comes with simply outlook for user friendly environment such as speech to text dictation, sharing of document via link, OneDrive cloud storage and lot more

Go to the "Font ribbon tab" beside your bold icon (**B**), click on **the italic icon (*I*)**

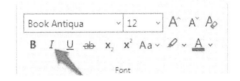

Then, your highlighted text will become italicized

Hello, this is Word 365 interface.

Word 365 interface comes with a lot of amazing features for Microsoft users with Word 365 you can share your document via link and track your progress with your team member.

Microsoft Word 365 also comes with simply outlook for user friendly environment such as speech to text dictation, sharing of document via link, OneDrive cloud storage and lot more

Superscript & Subscript

The **Subscript** button is used to write small letters just below the line of text. This tool is primarily used in Mathematics to differentiate between different variables. If you are conversant with Mathematics study and in any way have seen a variable like C_2, know that the "**2**" was made possible by the use of a subscript button/tool. In Word 365 environment, the subscript button is identified as x_2

The **Superscript** icon is the next after the subscript. The superscript button is used to write small letters just above the line of text. I firmly believe that you went through primary and secondary schools. Do you remember that time when you were taught **Indices**? Do you remember those times your teacher asked the class to give an answer to question 2^4 (pronounced as 2 to the power of 4)? That number **4** hanging on top of **2** is made possible using the superscript tool. The superscript icon is represented as x^2 in Word 365.

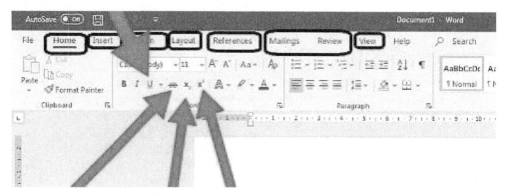

Let me assume that you have opened your Word 365 desktop application. I will then teach you how to apply these explained tools to get the expected result.

- To underline a few texts on Word 365, highlight the texts and then click the underline (U) button.
- To strikethrough words or letters, just highlight the word and then click the strikethrough button.
- If you want to apply subscript to any text or characters, first write the texts or characters (example C2), then highlight the text or number you want to subscript (in my given example of the two characters, I will highlight only "2"), and finally, click the subscript button. Once you do this, the letter will be below the main letter (for example, "2" will be below the "C" line).

To superscript any text contained in other texts, you have to highlight the text which you want to make superscript (for example, in text "K2," I have to highlight 2 because I want to make it superscript). After you have highlighted the letter/text which you want to make superscript, then click the **Superscript** icon. Once you do this, the text is made superscript.

Highlighting Text

A mouse can be used to select a block of text in major two perfect ways, either by dragging over the text or by clicking; we have to check the two ways for more understanding:

To make a text selection with the mouse dragging over, simply:

Locate where you want your selection to start from **and place your mouse cursor at that location.**

Immediately you place the cursor at the beginning of the spot and **drag the mouse over the text to the exact end** where you want to end the selection.

Excel is a spreadsheet application with the major purpose of organizing and carrying out the calculation on the data. It is a tool for recording, analyzing data and representing such data on a graph or chart.

Note: as you are dragging the mouse over the text, you will see the way the text is highlighting to the exact end where you release the mouse.

To make a text selection with the mouse clicking, I have never seen the fastest and most accurate means of selecting a block of text other than the mouse-clicking method; let us quickly check the mouse-clicking method:

Area Of The Text To Be Selected	Position And Action Of The Mouse
A single word	Double-click the mouse over any point within the word.

A line of the text	Go to the edge of the left margin of the line you want to select, and click the mouse cursor once on the edge.
A sentence	Place your mouse pointer to any spot within the sentence, hold down the Ctrl key, and left-click the mouse immediately. Such a sentence in the question will be highlighted.
A paragraph	Clicking any spot around a paragraph three times or click the left margin next to the paragraph twice to select the paragraph concerned.

Text Color

To change the look of your text, highlight your text.

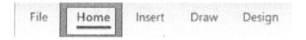

If your Word 365 interface is not on the "home tab" as its default display, simply go to the "home tab" and click on it.

Below the "home tab," select "font color," which is identified by a capital letter A underlined with a red stroke as illustrated with an arrow sign below. Are we together? Right, let us continue.

Remember that your text is still selected (highlighted). Once you click on "font color," your highlighted text will change to red color.

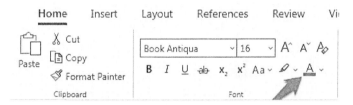

Choosing More Color

You can also click the little arrow beside the "font color" to select your preferred choice. If not found, check below for "more colors."

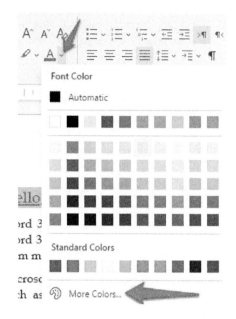

You can also decide to change the **"font style"** known as **"font name"** by selecting the **"home tab"** check on the little arrow beside your current font. Dropdown options will be displayed. You can select your preferred choice, but for similarity and understanding purpose, select **"Calibri Light (Headings)."**

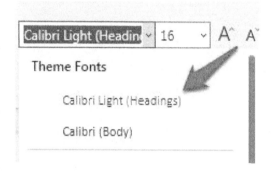

Your highlighted text will take effect immediately

Before

Hello, this is Word 365 interface.

After

Hello, this is Word 365 interface.

Text Justification

Paragraph alignment deals with the position of your text within a paragraph, whether it is to the left, right, or center, while the justification arranges your text neatly between the right and left margin and gives it a refined appearance, justification together with other alignments can be found in the Paragraph group under Home tab.

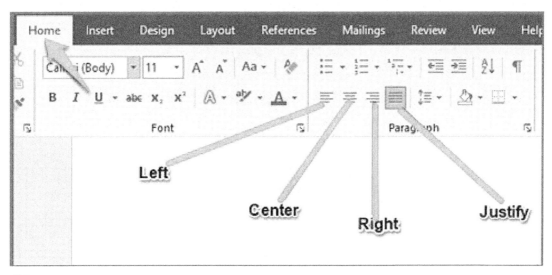

Left Alignment

Left alignment is used by the majority. According to research, out of 100 percent of the users, 70% will align their paragraph to the left, while the remaining 30% go for right and center alignment. To align the paragraph to the left side, kindly:

- Click the **left alignment command**. It is the first alignment on the paragraph group under the Home tab to align your paragraph to the left.

> Many people prefer PDF format of a document than the original word format of a document, though the universal acceptable format is that of the word format whether you are sharing a document on the web, saving it on the cloud or sending it to other via email, but some personality will specify PDF format for instance employer can specify your resume or CV to be in PDF format, to change word format to PDF, kindly study the guides below

- You may use shortcuts as well by pressing **(Ctrl + L).**

Center Alignment

Center alignment occupies the middle position or is centered between two edges, which is between the left and right alignment. This alignment is majorly used for Heading and subheading the pages. To center a text on the page, do well:

- Tap on the **center alignment command** and the second alignment on the paragraph group under the Home tab to center your text.

> Many people prefer PDF format of a document than the original word format of a document, though the universal acceptable format is that of the word format whether you are sharing a document on the web, saving it on the cloud or sending it to other via email, but some personality will specify PDF format for instance employer can specify your resume or CV to be in PDF format, to change word format to PDF, kindly study the guides below

- The shortcut for it is **(Ctrl + E).**

Right Alignment

Right alignment places the text on the right edge. The probability of seeing people aligning their work to the right is very slim. To right align a text on the page, take cognizance of the following:

- Tap on the **right alignment command**. It is the third alignment on the paragraph group under the Home tab.

- Right alignment shortcut is **(Ctrl + R).**

Justify Between The Left And Right Paragraph

This regulates the spacing by adding additional space between words and arranging them properly to occupy the entire line so that the alignment will be a balance between both left and right alignment. To justify a text on the page, kindly:

- Tap on the **justify command**. It is the last command inside the alignment section on the paragraph group under the Home tab.

> Many people prefer PDF format of a document than the original word format of a document, though the universal acceptable format is that of the word format whether you are sharing a document on the web, saving it on the cloud or sending it to other via email, but some personality will specify PDF format for instance employer can specify your resume or CV to be in PDF format, to change word format to PDF, kindly study the guides below

- The justified command shortcut is **(Ctrl + J).**

Note: this is the alignment used majorly in producing online textbooks and magazines.

Paragraph Indents

You may want to create a certain expression that will warrant you to indent the whole paragraph. Do you wish to indent an entire paragraph? Then do well to:

- Tap on the **Home tab** and maneuver to the paragraph group.

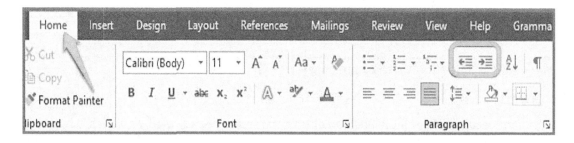

- Use **increase indent** to indent the paragraph. Increase Indentation will shift the paragraph to the front.

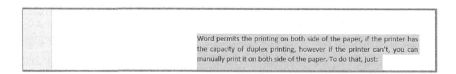

- **Decrease Indentation** will reverse or decrease the indented paragraph.

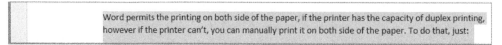

First Line Indent

When you indent the first line, the first line will shift forward from the margin while the rest line will remain unmoved, before people used to use the tab key to indent the first line. To indent the first line legally and in a modern way, kindly:

- Tap on the **Home tab or layout tab** and maneuver to the paragraph group.
- Click on the **paragraph dialog box launcher** to access the Paragraph dialog box.

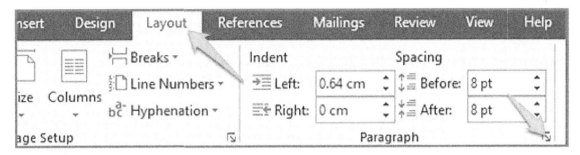

- **Within the dialog box, locate the** special button and tap on its down arrow, **and choose the** first line from the drop-down list.
- Use the **"By" button up and down** to set the indent space to 0.5 per normal indent space, which is the equivalent of a normal tab stop.

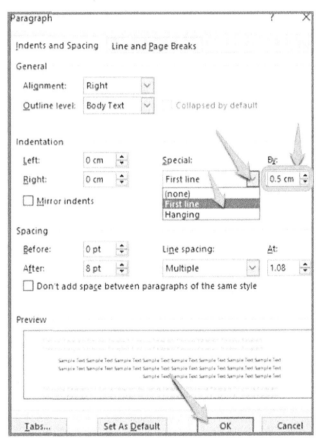

- Then tap **Ok.**

> Word permits the printing on both side of the paper, if the printer has the capacity of duplex printing, however if the printer can't, you can manually print it on both side of the paper. To do that, just:
>
> Once windows decide that your printer can't print on both, you will have to opt in for odd and even pages printing, and thus you will have to print both odd and even pages one after the other. To do that kindly:

Note: To clear the First line indent, follow the same processes as above. The only change is that of the special section. Instead of picking the first line, you would rather pick (none).

Hanging Indent

Hanging indentation, the opposite of the first-line indentation, is not always used to indent a document. You can find hanging indentations in indexes, bibliographies, and resumes. Hanging indentation makes other lines of the paragraph indented except the first line. To make a hanging indentation, do well:

- Click on the **paragraph launcher dialog box** from either the Layout or Home tab.
- **Tap on the** Special down arrow and choose Hanging, **then set the value with** the "By" box.

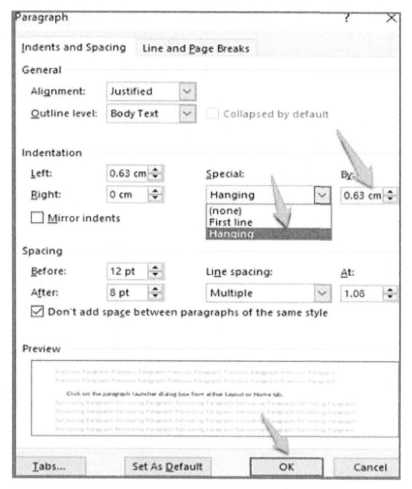

- Then tap **Ok.**

Note: the fastest way to create a hanging indent is to press (Ctrl + T), and you can reverse the hanging command by pressing (Ctrl + shift + T).

Paragraph Spacing

Adjusting The Space Between Paragraphs

- Go to the "Design tab"

- Look at your right-hand side and select "Paragraph Spacing"

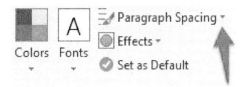

- A dialog box will appear displaying multiple options available for use

- Once you select your preferred choice, the effect will take place automatically on the entire document.

The Difference Between Line Spacing Under "Home Tab" & Paragraph Spacing Under "Design Tab"

- **Line and paragraph spacing under the** *"home tab"* adjust text manually, and it is done per paragraph, except you highlight the whole of your document.
- **Paragraph spacing under the** *"design tab"* adjusts text automatically. This affects the whole of your document.

Line Spacing

Adjusting The Space Between Lines

- Go to the "Home tab," which is Word 365 default displayed interface

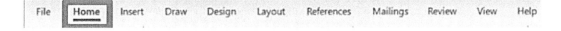

- On your right-hand side, locate "Paragraph ribbon" you will see the "line and paragraph spacing" icon

Paragraph

- Once you click in, you will be shown multiple options for line spacing between text or if your preferred choice is not in the list, click on "Line Spacing Options" to manually decide your choice

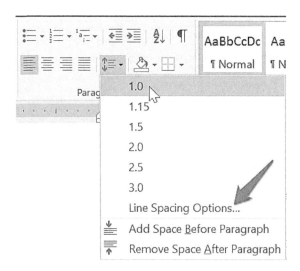

- If you click "Line Spacing Options" a dialog box will appear for you to decide your line spacing measurement. "Before" & "After" once set to your preferred choice, hit the "Ok" button below

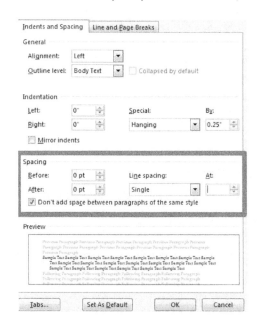

- It will automatically take effect on your opened document.

Tabs

The tab key is the shortened word for the word Tabulator key. The tab key is the cursor advancement to the next tab stop in the text, which represents the insertion of space characters with wide measurement compared to the spacebar. A tab stop is the limited space character to the next tab stop, and that is why you should set your tab stop appropriately when you use a tab key. Instead of striking a spacebar key twice or more. Your document will be arranged in order and accordingly. Just like the text and other characters, you can eliminate tab key characters with the use of the delete or spacebar key.

Viewing The Tab Character

You may view the tab character the way you use to view the text and other characters in the document. Tab character has an icon. Its icon is just like the shift icon but facing the right side. When you see a tab character, you can't do anything with it. You can only use it to adjust tab stop measurement.

To view tab character in a jiffy, quickly:

- Tap on the **show/hide command** in the Paragraph group under the Home tab.
- The **show/hide command** shows all special characters.

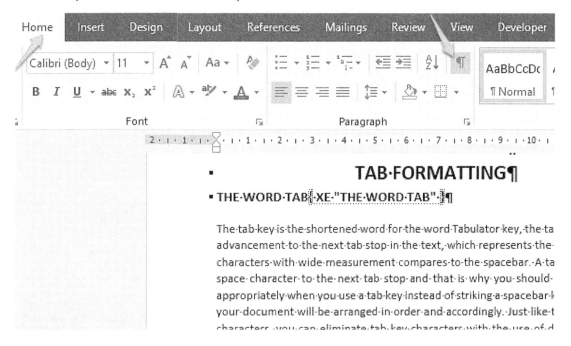

To view only the tab character in the text and ignore other characters, kindly:

- Tap on the **File and select the option** from the File backstage to access the Word Options dialog box.
- Pick **Display** from the left side of the Word Options dialog box.

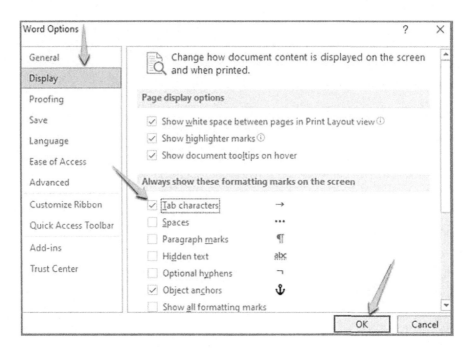

- Tick the **tab character option and tap on Ok**. As you click Ok, you will be referred back to your document, where you will be able to see the tab character icon.

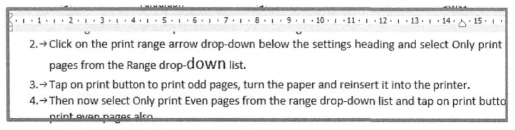

Setting And Adjusting The Tab Stops With The Ruler

You can't see tab stops in your document, but they affect any text you input after the striking of the tab key, which proves tab stops existence. To set and adjust the tab stop, you will have to make the tab stops visible by bringing out the ruler option. How? By:

- Tapping on the **View tab.**
- Locate the **show section and tick the ruler box**, provided it has not been ticked.

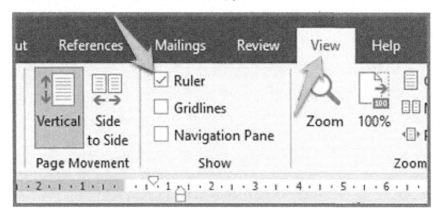

- Instantly, the ruler will come forth above the working area, and below the menu bar, it will show the Tab icon at the top of the vertical ruler and to the left of the horizontal ruler.

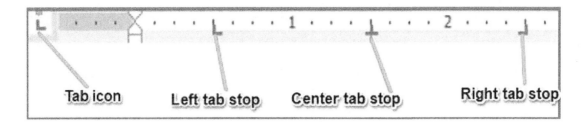

Tab icon   Left tab stop   Center tab stop   Right tab stop

Note: you may not see those tab stops until you set a tab stop. The tab stop that you are using may be a default tab, and the default tab does not use to be visible, but the tab icon is always available at the top of the vertical ruler and the left side of the horizontal ruler, which is what you will use to set the tab stop within the ruler.

To set the tab stop in your document, you will have to observe the following processes:

- **Continue clicking the tab icon** till it shows you the required tab stop, then move to the ruler side.
- **Single-click the actual position** on the ruler where you want the selected tab stops to set in. for instance. You may click 2 or 5 or 6 in the ruler, which will be the position where whichever tab stops set will be stopping.

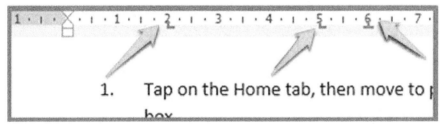

1.   Tap on the Home tab, then move to box

Note: anytime you set a tab stop, that tab stop will be visible on the ruler side, then you can drag it to adjust the settings of that particular tab stop. as you continue clicking the tab icon, you will see the two remaining tab stops, which are decimal and bar tabs. You can set as many tabs stops you want in a line.

Setting Tab Stops With Tabs Box Dialog Box.

To see all apparatus of tabs and all other tabs aside from left, center, and right tab such as decimal tab stops, you have to call for tabs dialog box. But remember, any time you want to set any tab stops when you are done with the setting, you should tap on **Set** then, after that you can tap Ok if you click on Ok million times without clicking on the set button, the tabs stop will not set. To summon the tabs dialog box and set a tabs stop, do well to:

- Tap on the **Home tab,** then move to paragraph group and click on **dialog box launche**r to open the paragraph dialog box.
- Click the **tabs button** inside the paragraph dialog box, and the tab dialog box will come forth.

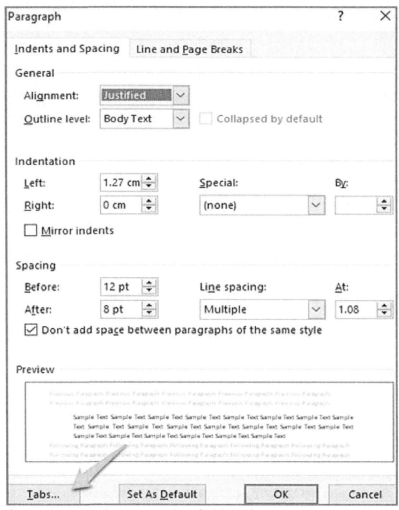

- Insert the **tab position** into the position box field, such as 2.5, depending on where you want your tab stops to set in.
- Select the **tabs stops type** you want in the alignment section.

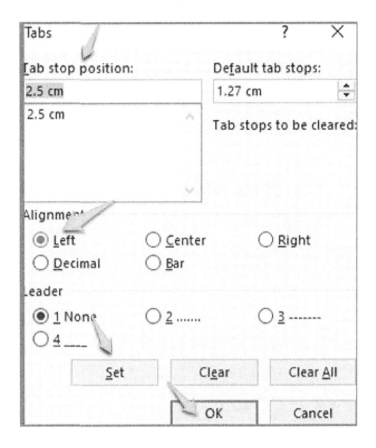

- Click on **Set,** and it will set immediately. You can use steps (2-5) above to set as many as possible tab stops, where the tab will be stopping on the line.
- After you have set all the tab stops you want in a line, then tap **Ok.**

Note: it is essential to click on set as you set each tab stop because, without that, tab stops will never be set.

Producing Two- A Tabbed List With Left Tab Stops

The left tab stop is majorly used in typing the text to move the cursor pointer to the front to another position of the left tab stop. Beyond that level, the left tab stop can as well be used to create a two-column tabbed list, even three tabbed lists. To create a list of two sides with a left tab stop, kindly study the below one on one guideline:

- Move to a new line, strike the **Tab key and insert the item** at most two to five words.
- Strike the **tab key a second time and insert the second** item also two to five words as well.

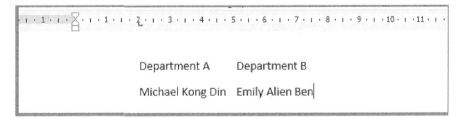

- Strike the **Enter key** to move to the next line and begin another line
- Repeat **steps (a-c)** to enter all the items for each of the lines in the list.

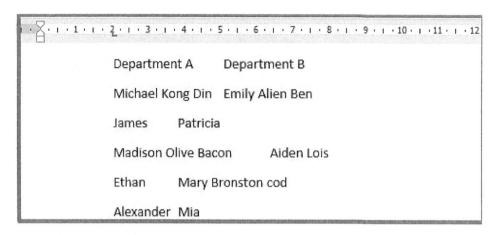

- **Highlight all the items** in the list that you want to arrange into the two-column and **move to the tab icon** at the top of the vertical rule and the left side of the horizontal ruler.

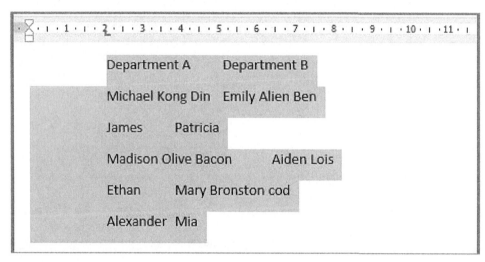

- **Continue clicking the tab icon** to set the tab icon to the left tab stop.

- Then move to the working area, and click the first position on the ruler measure, which will represent your first tab stop. For instance, 4 inch, you will see the reflection immediately.

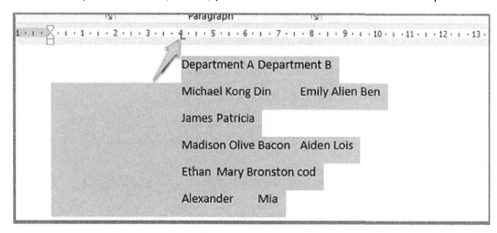

- Click on the second ruler's second position on the ruler measurement, which will represent your second tab stop. For instance, you may click 9inch depending on the width of the column. Behold! You have created a two-tabbed list.
- You can shift either or both tab stop to adjust the position of the tabbed stop if you wish. Shift it by double-clicking the tab stop and dragging it to the preferred location.

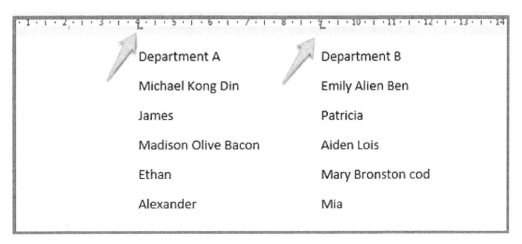

Note: you may as well use the left tab to prepare a three-tabbed list, but it depends on the details so that it will not be jam-packed.

Creating Tab Style With Leader Tabs

Leader tabs are not tabbed in an actual sense but are used to create a style for the tab's blank space. Instead of leaving a tab space blank, it is more attractive to add style. Leader style comes with 3 styles which are dot, dash, and underlines. How do I apply the leader tab to the tab blank space? This is the way, simply:

- Produce a tabbed list, just like the one we created above with a two-tabbed list.
- Select **all the items** in the tab list

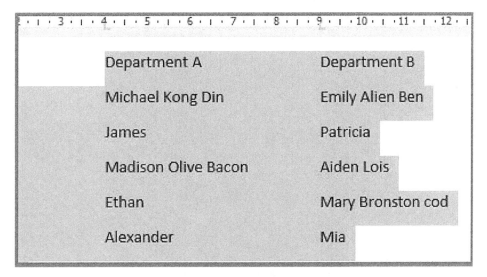

- Quickly send for tabs dialog box by simply **double-clicking on any tab stop** within the ruler area but if no tab stop is available, summon the tab stop dialog box from the paragraph dialog box by clicking on its launcher either from the Home or Layout launcher.

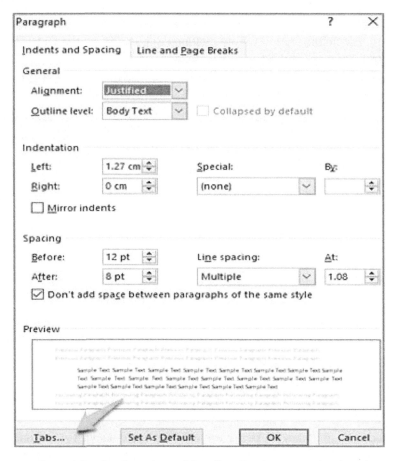

- Input the **exact tab position** in the tab position list. For instance, in the above tab list, the last tab stop, which is the blank space, is 9cm.
- Select your preferred **"leader style"** and tap on the **Set button.**

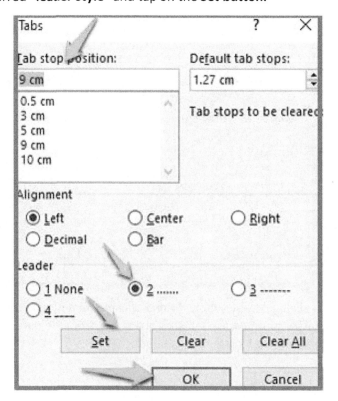

- Lastly, tap on **Ok**.

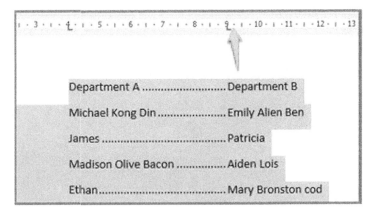

Clear A Tab Stop

You might set a tab stops wrongly, or you may not need it in your text anymore. To clear a tab stop, kindly:

- **Highlight the paragraph** that carries the tab stops you want to erase.
- Double-click on the tab stops **and** drag down **to clear any tab stops.**

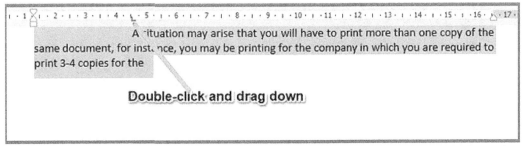

To clear multiple tab stops, perhaps the tab stops are not accurate and are affecting other tab stops. You may choose to clear all the tab stops. to clear all tab stops, kindly;

- Summon the tabs **dialog box.**
- Then **select any position** in the tap position list.
- Tap on the **Clear All button** and click Ok for verification.

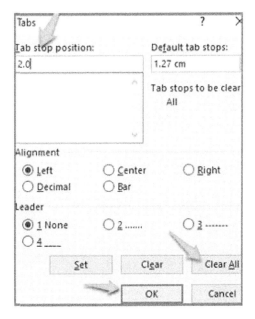

Note: when you tap on the Clear All button, all the tabs stop will be cleared.

Bullet Lists

Creating Bulleted Lists

- Highlight the portion of text that you want the bullet list to take effect on

- Go to the "Home tab," which is your display settings interface

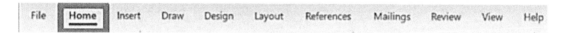

- On your left-hand side in the "Paragraph ribbon," the first tool you will see is the "Bullets list"

- In the "Bullet" list, select your preferred choice from your "bullet library" and click on it

- It will automatically take effect on your highlighted text

List of fruits
- ➢ Orange
- ➢ Apple
- ➢ Blueberry
- ➢ Watermelon
- ➢ Guava
- ➢ Banana

- Or you can click on "bullet list" and select your preferred choice on a free space in the document, which also grants you access to listing your item automatically.

List of fruits
➢

- Once you enter an item and you click on the "Enter key" from your keyboard, it will continue the bulleting automatically

List of fruits
- ➢ Orange
- ➢ |

Numbered Lists

List of fruits

Orange

Apple

Blueberry

Watermelon

Guava

Banana

Highlight the portion of text that you want the numbering list to affect

Go to the "Home tab," which is your display settings interface

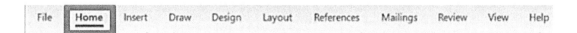

On your left-hand side, locate the "Paragraph ribbon," the second tool you will see beside the bullets icon is the "numbering list," click on it.

You will be given many options to pick from. You can pick the numbering of your choice.

Note: The numbering library consists of number listing, alphabet listing, and roman figure listing. It's not designed for numbers alone.

Immediately you select the number list (you can pick your preferred choice), and it will automatically take effect on your highlighted text.

List of fruits

1. Orange
2. Apple
3. Blueberry
4. Watermelon
5. Guava
6. Banana

Or you can check "number list" and select your preferred choice on a free space in your document, which also grants you access to listing your item automatically.

List of fruits

1. |

Once you enter an item and you click your "Enter key" on your keyboard, it will automatically continue the numbering.

List of fruits

1. Orange
2. |

Sorting Text

Sorting means an arrangement of a thing in a particular order. Sorting can sort an item or the text automatically for you. To sort the text, do well to:

- Put each item into a separate line and select them as a group.
- Tap on the **Home tab** and move to the paragraph section.

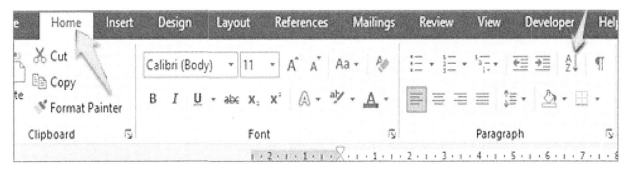

- Tap on **Sort commands** to open the Sort dialog box.

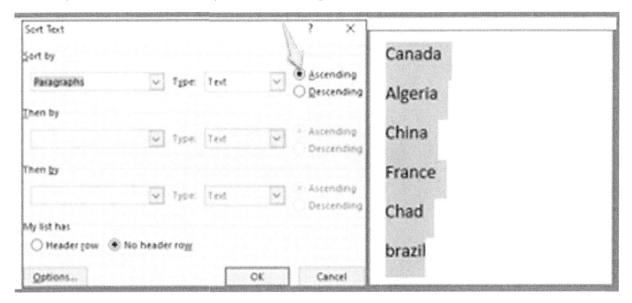

- Select **Ascending or descending,** depending on the order you prefer, and tap the Ok button

Algeria

Brazil|

Canada

Chad

China

France

Cut, Copy & Paste

Once you select a range of text (block), the such block can be moved or copied. Copying means retaining the original and duplicating it to another location while moving means taking away the original block to another location. Let us quickly check what it involves to move or copy a block:

- Select the **block of text** you want to move or copy.

> RELEVANCE OF EXCEL
>
> The relevancies of Excel cannot be overemphasized which makes it a preferable spreadsheet application over other spreadsheet programs, which is the key reason why it always finds expression in both small and big offices. To say the facts we can't talk about all Excel relevancies but we will touch over essential ones.

- Touch the **Home tab.**
- Move to the clipboard group and choose **copy or cut** for copying and moving, respectively.

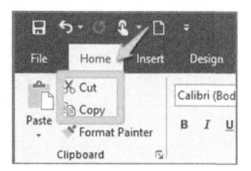

- Place the cursor pointer to the spot where you want to paste the block you have copied or cut above in (d).

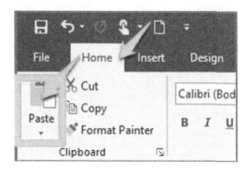

- Tap on the **paste command button** in the Clipboard group to paste the block you have copied or cut. In a jiffy, it will be pasted to the location where you place the cursor pointer.

> The relevancies of Excel cannot be overemphasized which makes it a preferable spreadsheet application over other spreadsheet programs, which is the key reason why it always finds expression in both small and big offices. To say the <u>facts</u> we can't talk about all Excel relevancies but we will touch over essential ones.
>
> The relevancies of Excel cannot be overemphasized which makes it a preferable spreadsheet application

Note: You can as well use the keyboard shortcut for cut and copy, which is (Ctrl + X) and (Ctrl + C), respectively. To paste an action with the cut and copy command, kindly press (Ctrl + V).

Tip: The texts you have cut or copied are on the clipboard, and therefore you can paste them as more as you want to the current or another document, even another program, until you cut or copy another command to the clipboard.

Using the Clipboard

The clipboard is the main storage of all the items you have cut and copied. Immediately you cut or copy the text, and it will be sent to the clipboard and will be there for some hours. The beauty of the clipboard is that any text you have cut or that you copy can be pasted again to your document at any location. To make exploitation from the clipboard, let us quickly delve into those steps:

- **Put the cursor pointer** to the place where you want to paste the cut or copy clipboard information.

> Excel 365 comes with a lot of benefits, but we will just make mention of the few
>
> (1) Instant communication in and out of the organization: Excel 365

Tap the **Home tab** and move to the clipboard group to click the dialog box launcher.

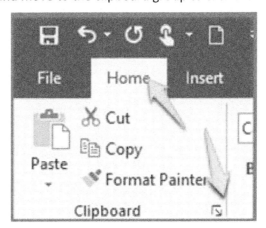

- Immediately you click **the clipboard dialog box launcher, the** clipboard task pane will come forth, then place the mouse pointer at any text or image you want to paste from the clipboard task pane, and instantly a menu drop-down at the right of the text or information.
- Tap on the **menu drop-down button and select the paste command.** In a jiffy, it will be pasted to the spot will you place the cursor pointer in (a) above.

Inserting Symbols

There are various "special characters and symbols" embedded in the insert tab. To access them, kindly:

- Tap on the **insert tab** and move to the symbols section at the right end.

Tap on the **symbols menu** to access some symbols and special characters.

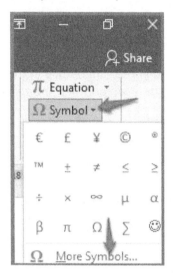

- Search through the field symbol to select special characters and symbols. If you can't find them here, simply tap on more symbols to go to the main field of symbols, where all symbols and characters dwell.

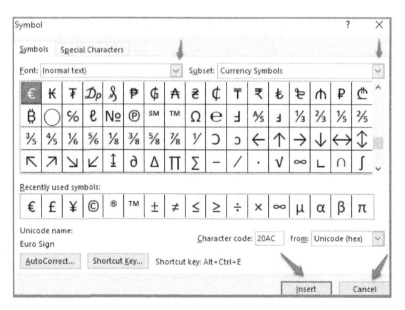

Note: to insert any symbols click on the symbol and tap on insert. When you are done using the symbols menu, tap on cancel.

Tips: tap on Font and subset to see other sections of symbols and special characters. Perhaps the symbols and characters you are finding are not among the listed.

Hidden Characters

Tap on the **Home tab** and maneuver to the paragraph section, then tap on the **show/hide command button** to make every hidden character visible.

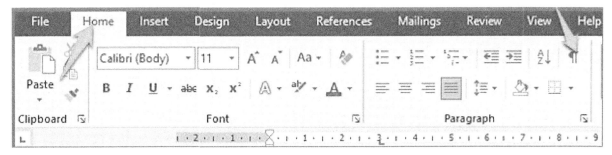

Equations

You can perform complex mathematical equations such as polynomial, binomial and other equations. To achieve this, simply:

- Tap on the **Insert tab** and move to the symbols section far right of the screen.

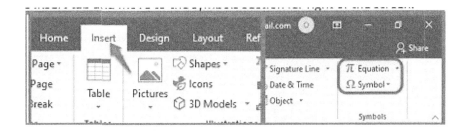

- Click on the **equation button** and select the **equation** you want to use from the list, the equation will come up from the spot where you place the cursor pointer.

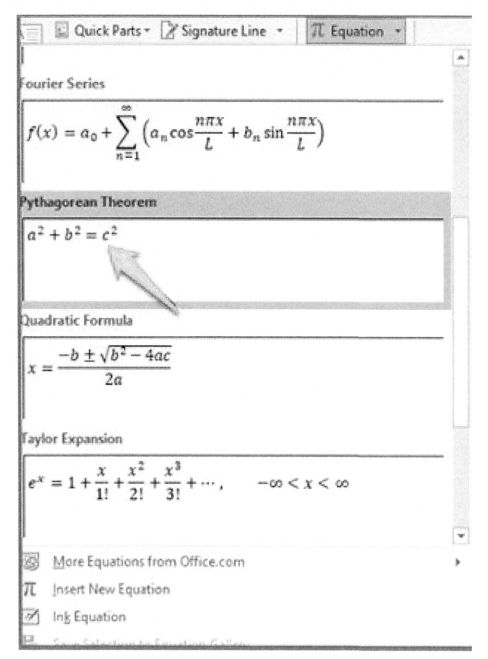

- Then change the equation format by using the numbers to replace the letter.

Note: word can give you millions of equation formulas but will not calculate for you.

Chapter 4: **Saving Documents**

How To Save A Document Directly To Your PC?

- Go to "File menu"

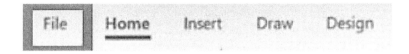

- Select "Save option"

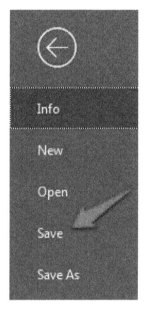

A dialog box will appear, select the location you want to save, name your document on the "File name box" and click "Save".

Note: saving your document on your PC is only for licensed users, Microsoft Word online free version saves automatically online on OneDrive storage.

How To Save A Document Directly To Your OneDrive Cloud Storage?

- Go to "file menu"

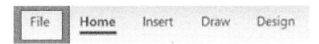

- You will see multiple options, select "Save as"

- A dialog box will appear, you will see the "OneDrive" option, once you click it, your document will be saved online. If you have many folders on your OneDrive storage, you will be asked to choose the destination you want your work to be saved in. Once done, hit "Save".

Saving as a Different Format

Many people prefer the PDF format of a document to the original word format of a document. However, the universal acceptable format is that of the word format whether you are sharing a document on the web, saving it on the cloud, or sending it to others via email, some people will specify PDF format. For instance, employer can specify that your resume or CV to be in PDF format, to change word format to PDF, kindly study the guides below:

- Update the current changes by saving your document once more either with Ctrl + S or other means.
- Tap on **Print** from the File tab backstage to send for the print screen.
- Tap on the **printer menu** to access the list of available printers.
- Select **Microsoft Print to PDF** and tap on the **Print button**. It will not print anything but you will be transited to the Save Print Output As dialog box.

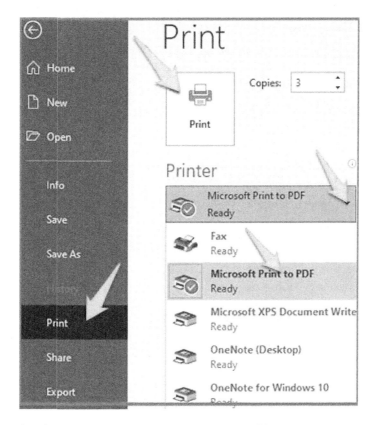

- **Select a** file location for the NEW PDF document **and insert a** file name.
- Tap on the **Save button** to create the PDF file.

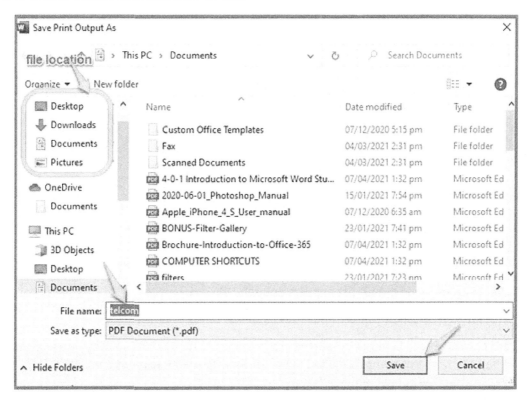

Note: when you print a document out from the printer, the original document remains untouched likewise when printing PDF format, it will not change anything from the original document that you converted into PDF. You can open and edit PDF files the same way you edit MS word documents.

Opening Saved Documents

You can open your document from the Word application or directly from your device.

To open an existing document from Word:

- Go to the backstage view by clicking on the **File** tab.
- Click the **Open** tab.
- **Open** pane appears.
- Select the location of your document.
- An **Open** dialog box appears.
- Select the folder or your document. You can scroll down the left side list of locations on your device to locate your document.
- Click **Open**.

Alternatively, if you recently opened your document or pinned it to Word, it will be available in the **Recent** or **Pinned** list in the backstage **Home** panel, and you can click on it to open it.

If you often use or work on your document, it will be better to pin it in Word.

To pin your document to the word:

- Locate the document in the recent list.
- Move your cursor over the document.
- Click the pin icon in front of the file.

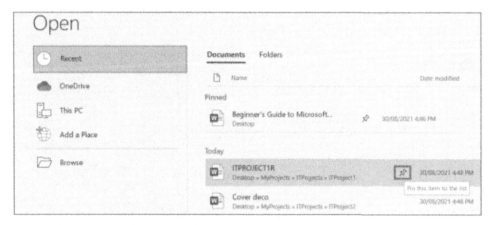

To open an existing document from your device:

- Ensure you have the Word application installed on your computer.
- Locate your Word document on your device.
- Double-click to open it if it has a Word icon, if not, right-click on the file.

Select **open with** from the menu that appears and select **Word**.

Sharing Documents

Your word document can be easily shared directly as an email body or as an attachment to an email address with the **Send to Mail Recipient** command in Word. **Send to Mail Recipient** command is not available in the Word user interface by default and needs to be added. You can preferably add it to the Quick Access Toolbar by customizing it.

To add 'Send to Mail Recipient' to Quick Access Toolbar (QAT):

- Right-click on the **QAT**.
- A dialog box appears.
- Select **Customize Quick Access Toolbar**.

- Word Options dialog box appears.
- From the **Choose commands from** the drop-down list, choose **Commands Not in the Ribbon**.
- Locate **Send to Mail Recipient** in the list. The list is arranged alphabetically for easy location.
- Click **Add>>** button.
- Word adds it to Customize Quick Access Toolbar.
- Click **OK,** and it appears in your Quick Access Toolbar.

To share your document as an email body:

- Ensure your computer is connected and sign in to your email account.
- Click on **Send to Mail Recipient** command in the Quick Access Toolbar.
- The mail Composing window appears under the ribbon with your document title already added.
- Add the recipient's email address and other information as desired. You can also change the title as desired.
- Ensure you have an internet connection.
- Click **Send a Copy**.

Word sends your document and closes the composing email window. To close the email window manually, click on the icon in the Quick Access Toolbar.

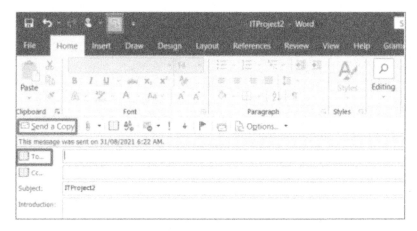

Chapter 5: **Printing Documents**

Printing a document is the result of creating and saving a document, printing is not just printing through a hard copy alone, it also involves distributing the information online so that every potential user can have access to it.

The print preview gives you an outlay to view how the document will be presented or the result you are likely to get and use that as a yardstick to decide if there will be any adjustments such as a blank page and another editing before printing. How do I preview a document? That should not be a problem, kindly:

- Click on the **File tab and choose Print** from the File backstage or press **Ctrl + P** to summon the Print screen box.
- **Use the** zoom controller to increase or decrease **the look of the document.**
- Switch throughout the pages in the document with the switch button at the bottom of the print screen, if you want to apply any editing click on the back arrow or Esc to return to the document and make the necessary adjustment.

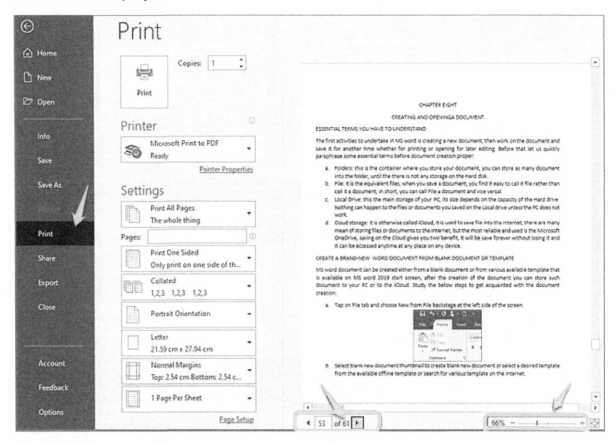

Printing The Whole Document

To print all the pages of your document, study the following steps:

- Save the document by pressing **Ctrl + S,** then "ON" the printer, and insert the papers.
- **Click the** File tab and select print or press Ctrl + P.
- Then tap on **the print button,** immediately print screen will dismiss and the document will be coming forth from the printer.

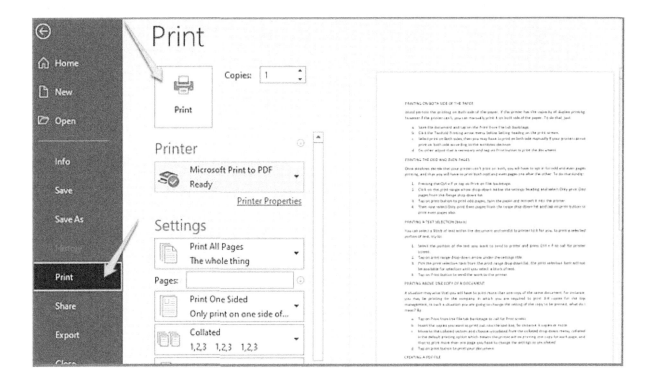

Note: if the printer does not begin printing immediately, do not press the print command again not to end up printing more than a necessary document, wait patiently. It depends on how fast each printer works.

Some documents are structured in such a way that they will specify the type of paper needed to print them, and thus endeavor to insert the suitable paper any time the document request such a thing.

Printing An Exact Page

There may be a demand to print an exact page, perhaps one of the pages printed got missing or any other reason, and thus you will be left with an option to print that very page alone. To print the exact page out of the whole document, look at these steps;

- **Maneuver to that exact page** and ensure that the cursor pointer is at that very page by checking the status bar to confirm if you are at that definite page, for instance, page 8.

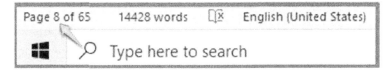

- Tap on **File and click on print** from backstage.
- Click on the **print range arrow drop-down** right below the settings heading.

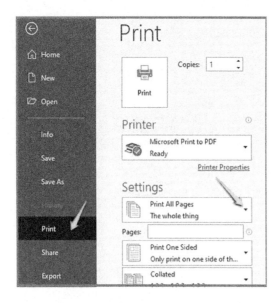 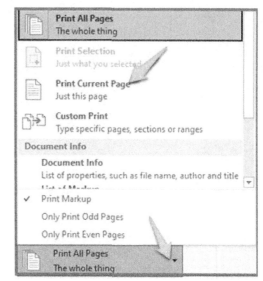

- Select Print current page from the print range drop-down menu.
- **Tap on the** print button.

Note: it will print the specified page per the whole formatting of the whole document.

Printing Range Of Pages

You can print choices of any pages, whatever range of any type, including even and odd pages. To print choices of pages kindly bring forth the print screen by:

- Pressing the **Ctrl + P or tap on Print** on the File backstage.
- Click on the **print range arrow drop-down** below the settings heading.
- Select the **custom page** from the print range drop-down to activate the range box.
- Below the print range is the range box, insert the **exact range** you want your printer to print out into the range box, such as 2-5 for printing page 2 through to page 5, or 6-7 and 8, and 10-14 for printing page 6 through to 7, and page 8 then page 10 through to 14, depending on the choice of pages you want to print.
- Tap on the **Print button** to send the range of documents to the printer.

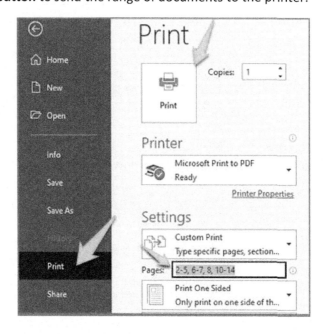

Printing On Both Sides Of The Paper

Word permits the printing on both sides of the paper if the printer has the capacity of Twofold printing, however, if the printer does not, you can manually print it on both sides of the paper. To print on both sides of the paper, just:

- Save the document and tap on the Print **from File tab backstage.**
- Click the **One-sided heading arrow menu** below the Setting heading on the print screen.

- Select **print on Both sides with flip pages on the long side**, you may choose flip pages on the short side if you want to bind the document, provided your printer can print twofold, but if it can't print on both sides, you will have to choose manual print on both sides but you will have to reload paper when next you want to Print on the second side.

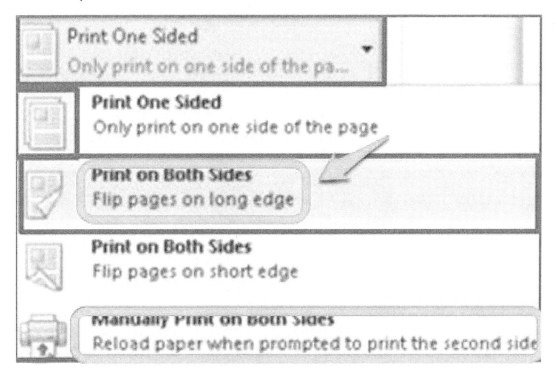

- Carry out other adjustments that are necessary and tap on the **Print button** to print the document.

Note: the decision of whether the printer can print on both sides is the sole right of the window, not the decision of the program you are running.

Printing The Odd And Even Pages

Once windows decide that your printer can't print on both sides, some users prefer to use the odd and even method rather than choosing manual printing, and thus you will have to print both odd and even pages one after the other. To do that kindly:

- Pressing the **Ctrl + P or tap on Print** on File backstage.
- Click on the **print range arrow drop-down** below the settings heading and select Only Odd print pages from the Range drop-down list.

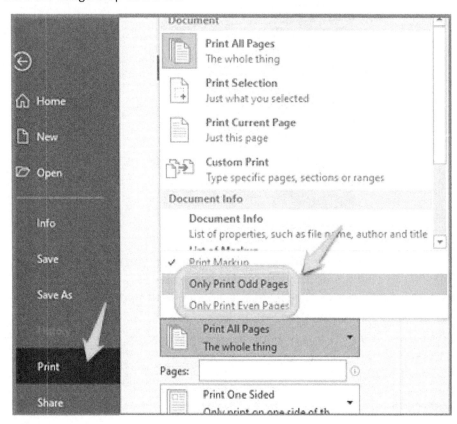

- Tap on the **print button to print odd pages,** turn the paper and reinsert it into the printer.
- Then now **select Only print Even pages** from the range drop-down list and tap on the print button to print even pages also.

Note: you will print the odd pages first then follow the same procedure to print the even pages as well.

Printing A Text Selection (Block)

You can select a block of text within the document and send it to the printer to print a selected portion of text, try to:

- Select the **portion of the text** you want to send to the printer and tap on **Print** from the File backstage to call for the printer screen.

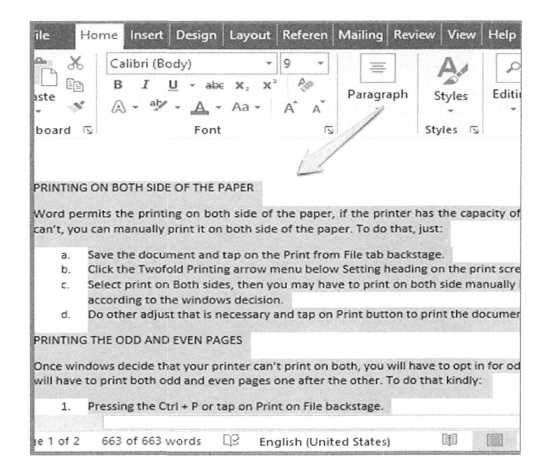

PRINTING ON BOTH SIDE OF THE PAPER

Word permits the printing on both side of the paper, if the printer has the capacity of can't, you can manually print it on both side of the paper. To do that, just:

a. Save the document and tap on the Print from File tab backstage.
b. Click the Twofold Printing arrow menu below Setting heading on the print scre
c. Select print on Both sides, then you may have to print on both side manually according to the windows decision.
d. Do other adjust that is necessary and tap on Print button to print the documer

PRINTING THE ODD AND EVEN PAGES

Once windows decide that your printer can't print on both, you will have to opt in for od will have to print both odd and even pages one after the other. To do that kindly:

1. Pressing the Ctrl + P or tap on Print on File backstage.

- Tap on the **print range drop-down arrow** under the settings title.
- Pick the **print selection item** from the print range drop-down list, the print selection item will not be available for selection until you select a block of text.
- Tap on the **Print button** to send the work to the printer.

Printing Above One Copy Of A Document

A situation may arise that you will have to print more than one copy of the same document, for instance, you may be printing for the company in which you are required to print 3-4 copies for the top management, in such a situation you are going to change the setting of the copy to be printed, what do I mean? By:

- Tap on **Print from the File tab backstage** to call for the Print screen
- Insert the **copies** you want to print out into the text box, for instance, 3 copies or more.

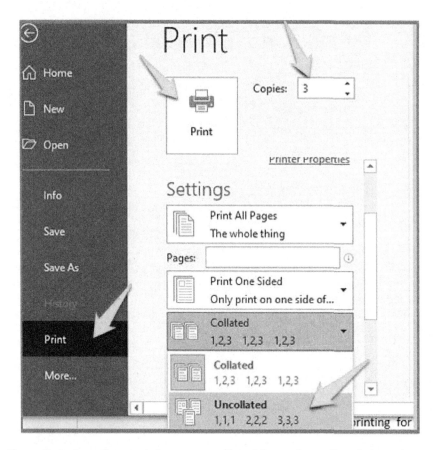

- Move to the **collated section** and choose **uncollated** from the collated drop-down menu, collated is the default printing option which means the printer will be printing one copy for each page, and thus to print more than one page, probably between 3- 5 pages, you will have to change the settings to uncollated.
- Tap on the **print button** to print your document.

Chapter 6: **Page Setup**

A page is a complete portion of a document that equals what you can print out as whole information. There is major formatting to be carried out on the page before it will be qualified to be called a proper page, such as page margin, orientation, and lots more.

Setting Your Page Size

Page size is the actual measurement that looks like a booklet, this is the room that will accommodate the text you inserted into the document. There are different sizes of paper, you can select any one depending on the type of document you are making, for instance, legal paper, A4 paper, and so on. To pick a certain page size or change the one you are using currently, kindly:

- Tap on the **layout tab** and maneuver to the page setup section.
- Tap on the **size button-down arrow** from the page setup section and select **your desired page size**.

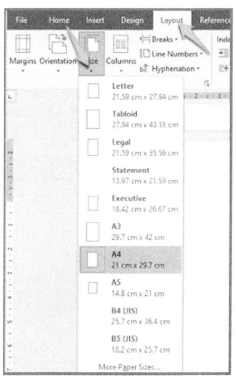

Note: the page size you selected will have a reflection by the time of printing, and you can't just choose paper anyhow unless your printer can print different paper aside from the one selected in printing a document. The paper you selected is a copy of how your whole document will appear.

Changing From One Page Orientation To Another

Page orientation has to do with whether the page is positioned landscape or portrait when the document is on landscape orientation, it means the page is horizontally based (it has more horizontal length than its vertical length), while the portrait-oriented is vertical based (its vertical length is more than its horizontal length). To change from one orientation to another, kindly:

- Tap on the **layout tab** and maneuver to the page setup section.
- Click on the **orientation down arrow** and select either **Portrait or landscape** on the menu drop-down depending on the one you are having or using before because page orientation has only two options and that is Portrait and landscape.

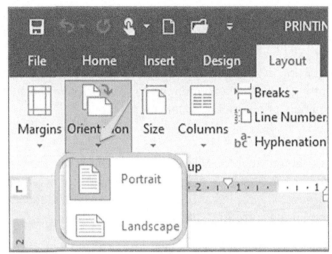

Note: Ensure you select the actual orientation for your document from the beginning, changing orientation from a text-filled document can be so frustrating by disorganizing the entire document and changing the paragraph formatting. However, you can have a separate orientation in a document by splitting the document into two sections with a page break depending on what you want to use the document to do.

Setting The Page Margin

Margin is the edge or border that encloses the text, it is the four borders of the page that is the top, bottom, right, and left edge of the page. if you set your margin accurately, you will see your text sitting on the Page properly. To select a page margin, do well to:

- Tap on the **layout tab** and maneuver to the page setup section.
- Click on the **margin down arrow** and select an **appropriate margin**. Margin is all about four options, given you the option to select the actual space your text space that will remain on four sides of the margin, the type of margin you select will determine the space you will be having at the four edges of the page.

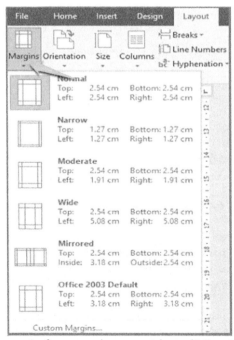

Note: you can select a different margin for your document by splitting the document into sections with a page break.

Command Page Setup Dialog Box For Page Setting

Page set up dialog box permits you to access all page setting in a single room and give you more access to further page setting. To access the page setup dialog box, examine the procedures to call it out:

- Tap on the **layout tab** and maneuver to the page setup section

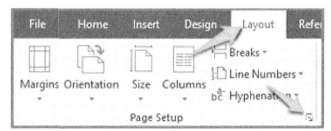

- Click on the **page setup dialog box launcher** to bring forth the page setup dialog box.
- Insert the margin values to the respective four sides (top, bottom, left, and right) in the provided field.
- Select if you want to apply the setting to the **whole document or from this point forward.**

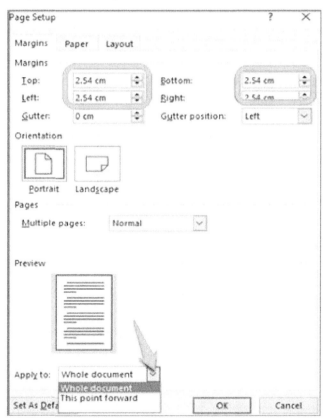

- Input all the settings you want and tap Ok for verification.

Note: click on either of the three-tab of the page setup box to adjust your settings (Margin, paper, and layout). The gutter option under the margin section deals with additional space for whatever edges you selected, for instance, project work usually has binding at the left side, you can use gutter to provide a house for the binding space without touching the text.

Adding Auto Page Number

MS word grants you the chance to insert page numbers into your document automatically, instead of numbering it one after the other page by page. You can use different formats for page numbering from the various number format from MS words, such as Arabic and Roman numerals. With much ado, let us dive into numbering pages automatically:

- Tap on the **insert tab** and navigate to Header and Footer section.

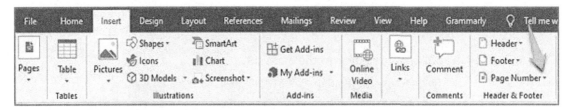

- **Tap on the Page number down arrow** and select the **actual position** (top or bottom) where you want to lay your page numbers.

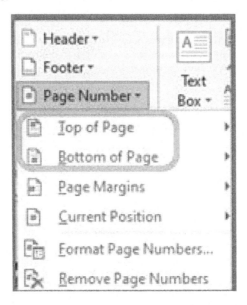

- Click on the **side arrow** of any of the options you made in (2) above to select the numbering style. You may scroll down if you have not yet gotten the preferable numbering style.

Note: instantly you select numbering style, Automatically MS word will number your document beginning with the first page as number 1, irrespective of the page number position you are in the document. Any adjustment you made in the document, the MS word we renumber for you, for instance, if you add or remove any page, word automatically renumbers the remaining pages for you.

Starting Page Numbering With Any Number

Anytime you are numbering a document, MS word starts from the first page with number one, However, you can dictate for MS word to start the first page by any number of your choice, for instance, you can start from number 60 depending on the situation. How will you do that? By:

- Tap on the **Insert tab** and maneuver to the Header and Footer section.
- Click on the **Page number down arrow** and **select Format page numbers** from the drop-down list to open the Page number format dialog box.

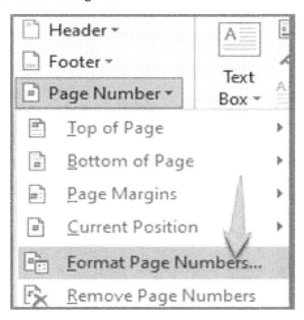

- **Tick on the "Start at" small circle** to select it and then insert the **exact number** where you want your document to start from.

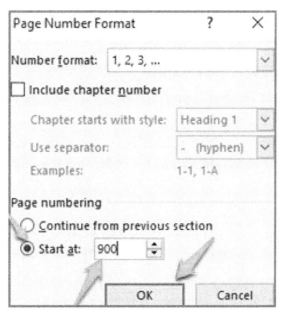

- Tap Ok for verification.

Note: if you type that your number should start with 900 at the start, the first page of the document will be 900, followed by 901 and the subsequent page will increase in that order.

Numbering With Another Format (Roman Numerals Or Alphabets)

Word number a figure with the normal number, you can dictate specific or change the numbering format for MS word, simply by:

- Tap on the **Insert tab** and maneuver to the Header and Footer section.
- Click on the **page number down arrow** and select **Format page number** from the drop-down list to open the Page number format dialog box.
- Tap on the **Number format menu** and select an appropriate style for your document in the dialog box.

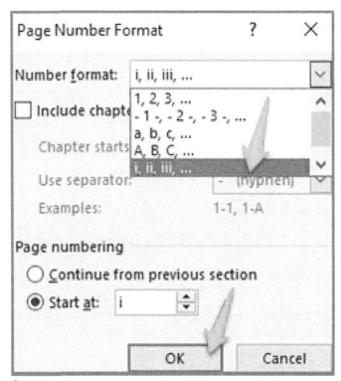

- Tap on **Ok** for verification.

Removing Page Numbers Of Any Kind

Perhaps you do not need a page number in your document or you have selected a wrong page number, quickly chase it out from your document with these little tricks:

- Tap on the **insert tab** and maneuver to the Header and Footer setting.
- Click on the **Page number down arrow** and select **Remove Page number** to send the page number out of the document.

Adding Text To A New Page

Text can be easily added to a new page at the end of the document, but what if the situation requires you to enter a text at the middle or the top of the document? You do not have to stress yourself about that, simply follow this little trick:

- Place the cursor pointer to the spot where one page ends and another one page to begin, suitably at the beginning of the first paragraph on the page.

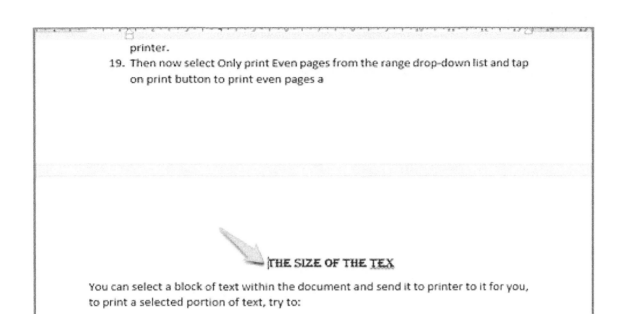

printer.

19. Then now select Only print Even pages from the range drop-down list and tap on print button to print even pages a

THE SIZE OF THE TEX

You can select a block of text within the document and send it to printer to it for you, to print a selected portion of text, try to:

- Tap on the **insert tab** and maneuver to the page section and tap on the **Break page.**

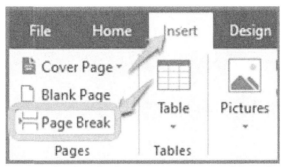

- Behold! A new page has come forth, whichever text you typed into the page will never affect the text of any page previously before it, if the text is more than a page another page will come forth without tampering with another section.

Note: a new page will come forth, the page above the cursor pointer will come above this new page while the page before the cursor pointer will come below the new page, this command is called a hard break, you can undo the hard page break with Ctrl + Z).

Adding A Blank Page

You can as well add a blank page within a document, but anytime the blank page is full it will shift the text in the previous page before its creation, and therefore adding a blank page is recommended for something that will not exceed a page such as a table or any image. To create a blank page within a document, do well to:

- Tap on the **Insert tab** and maneuver to the page group.
- Then tap on the **Blank page command button** to insert a new blank page.

Note: a new blank page will come forth, the page above of cursor pointer will come above the new blank page while the page before the cursor pointer will come below the new blank page, this command is called two hard breaks, you can also undo two hard pages with (Ctrl + Z).

Multiple Documents

Viewing files through more than one Window creates the possibility to work in another Window and not affect your original Window.

Steps on how to apply it:

View

From your current opened document, go to "View menu bar" by your right-hand side.

It is advisable to purchase a license Microsoft Office installation software because the one online is still very much under progressive development; not all features are on Word 365 web base.

New
Window

Under the "view menu bar", click on "New Window" (which is known as document interface), your current document which is opened will be duplicated and named "document 1" by default, except you rename it. Another duplicated one will be named "document 2"

Document 1 - Saved to OneDrive ⌄

Document 2 - Saved to OneDrive ⌄

Any changes in one will automatically lead to the same changes in the other.

Chapter 7: **Layout**

Putting Header on Pages

- Go to "Insert tab"

- At your right-hand side, look for "Header"

- A dialog box will appear, select your preferred alignment positioning

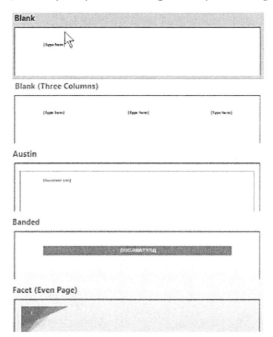

- Once done, you will be brought to your header editing edge to input your text

Word Handles Text Better

Note: You can also double-click on the top empty edge of your document to make use of the header format.

Removing Header from Pages

- Go to "Insert tab"

- At your right-hand side, locate "Header" and click on it

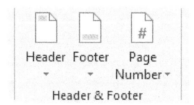

- A dialog box will appear below "Header" showing you header positioning, look down the list you will see "Remove Header". Once you click on it, your "Header" will be removed automatically

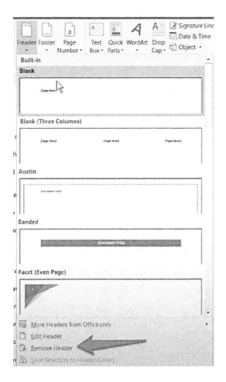

Putting Footer on Pages

- Go to "Insert tab"

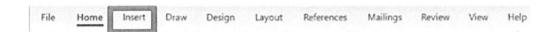

- At your right-hand side, locate "Footer" and click on it

- A dialog box will appear, select your preferred alignment positioning

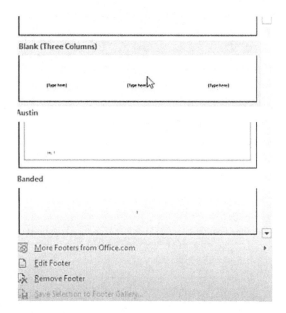

Once done, you will be brought to your footer editing edge to input your text

and rows to huge tables with hundr

supports tables it cannot handle large t

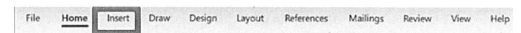

Note: You can also double-click below the page you want to insert the footer, you will be brought to an empty or footer format area where you can input your footer format.

Removing Footer from Pages

- Go to "Insert tab"

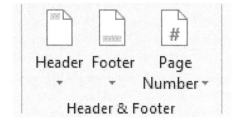

- At your right-hand side, locate "Header", click on it
- A dialog box will appear below "Footer" showing you footer positioning, look down the list, you will see "Remove Footer". Once you click on it, your "Footer" will be removed automatically

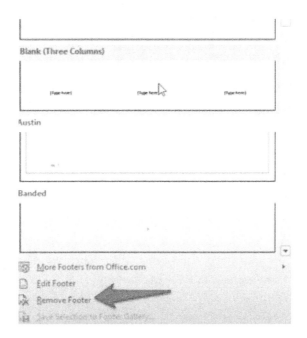

Page Numbering

Page Numbering is a way of making your content arranged serially for orderliness and reference purposes.

How to Insert Page Numbering

- Go to "Insert tab"

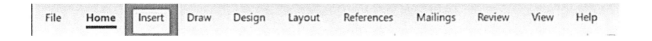

- At your right-hand side, you will see "Page Number" under "Header & Footer ribbon"

- Click on "Page Number", once you click on it, you will be given multiple options on where you want your page numbering to be positioned such as "Top of Page", "Bottom of Page", "Page Margins", "Current Position".

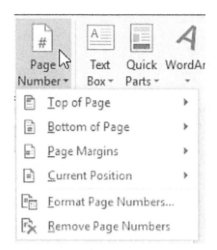

Or you can decide how you want your page numbering to look by clicking on "Format Page Numbers". A dialog box will appear for you to configure your Page Numberings such as "Number format", where you want to start effecting from, and lots more. Once you fill it, press "ok" to effect changes

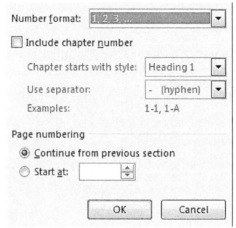

- Assuming you want the "Bottom of Page" option, click on "Bottom of Page" which is the normally used page numbering
- A dialog box will appear beside it, choose the middle numbering format

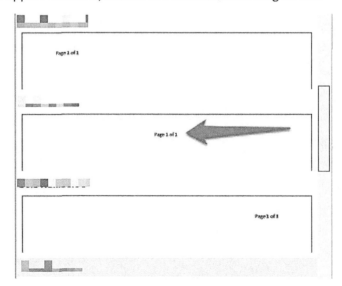

- By default, all your text will automatically be numbered serially

Remove Page Numbering

- Go to "Insert tab"

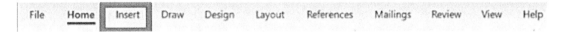

- At your right-hand side, you will see "Page Number" under "Header & Footer ribbon"

- Click on "Page Number", once you click on it, you will be given multiple options, look for "Remove Page Numbers", click on it, and every page numbering on your current opened document will be removed automatically

Page Borders

- Go to the "Design" tab

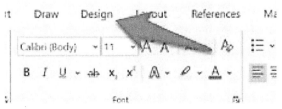

- Under "Design", at your right-hand side, you will see the "Page Background" ribbon, select "Page Borders"

81

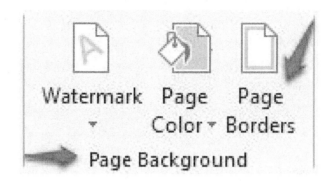

- Once you click on "Page Borders", a dialog box will pop up which is your "Page Border" configuration. On the left-hand side is the "Setting" option for various page border templates. By the side of the "Setting" option is the "Style" option where you can choose the kind of lines you prefer. Below "Style" is the "Color" option where you can determine which color fits into your page document border.

Below the "Color" option is the "Width" option which is the only component that controls the border thickness. Below the "Width" option is the "Art" option that reflects different kinds of art designs to be used for your framework, while at your right-hand side is the "Preview" option which gives you what your outcome configuration will look like before you click on the "Ok" option.

The "Apply to" option is where you determine where your effect should take place such as "Whole document", "This section", "This section first page only", and "This section all except the first page." Your choice determines your outcome, once done hit the "Ok" button to see your changes.

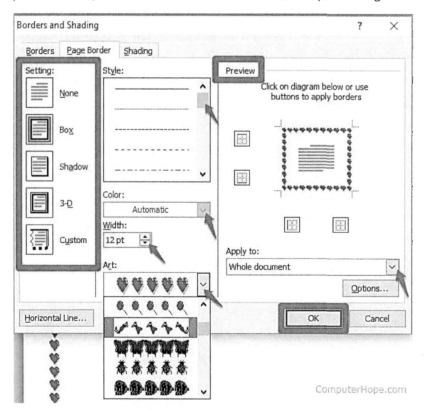

Page Breaks

Page break separates the content between pages. When the page break is inserted, the text starts at the beginning of the page.

To insert a page break in your document, follow the steps below

Click on where you want to insert the section break

Go to the **Layout** tab and click on the **Breaks** button

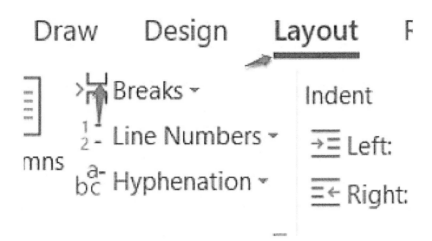

In the Break drop-down list, select any of the following options

- Page: This marks the point at which one page ends and the next page begins.
- Column: This specifies the text following the column break that will begin in the next column.
- Text Wrapping: This separates text around objects on web pages, such as captions from text from the body text.

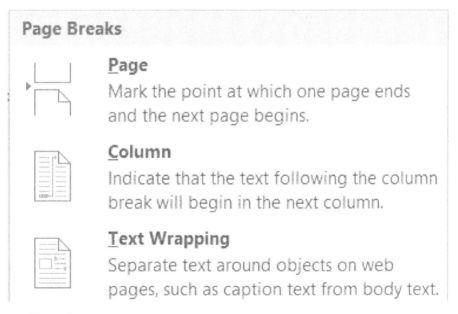

Deleting Page Break

To delete the page break inserted into your document, the first thing you need to do is ensure that the page break dotted line is visible in the document. If it is not, go to the **Home** tab, in the **Paragraph** group, and click on **Show or Hide**

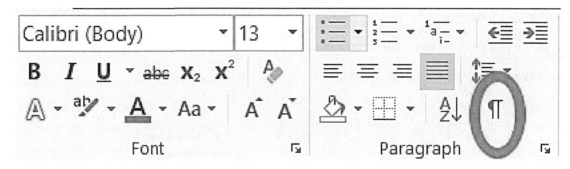

Change the view of your document to Draft view so that you can see where the section line is inserted. Click on the dotted line, and then press the Delete

~~Home tab, click the down arrow on the Dictate button~~
regional·language·from·the·drop-down·list.¶
Place·the·cursor·where·you·want·the·words·to·appear

------------------------------- Page Break ------------------------------- ¶

dictate·to·Word,·PowerPoint,·or·Outlook:¶

—

Creating Columns

The rows or row columns or both may not be enough or more than required, it depends on the situation. To add rows or columns, do well to:

- Place the cursor pointer to the left or right of the rows or columns where you want the new row or column to stay.
- Then tap on the **table tool layout tab** and move to the rows and columns section.

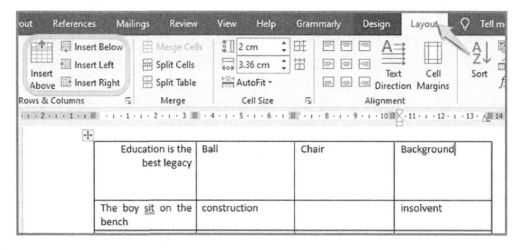

- Use the **insert button command** to add the respective row and column.

To remove the rows or columns, just:

- Select the row or column to be removed and move to the row and column section.
- Then tap on the **delete menu** and select the **proper delete option.**

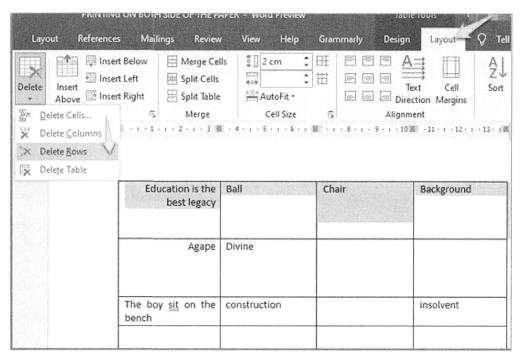

Note: To delete a cell, you will have one more option, you will decide the position of the neighbor cells before any cell will be removed.

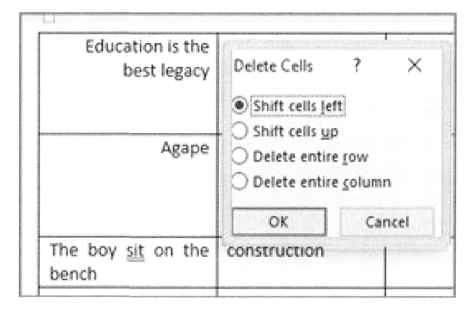

Adding Rows Or Columns With A Mouse

To add a new column, move the mouse pointer to the top edge at the very side where you want the new column to come forth and shift the cursor till you see the plus icon inside the circle, click it and a new column will come forth.

Education is the best legacy	Ball	Chair	Background	
Agape	Divine			
The boy sit on the bench	construction		insolvent	

To add a new row, move the mouse pointer to the left edge at the side where you want the new row to come forth and shift the cursor till you see the plus icon inside a circle, click it and a new row will come forth.

Adjusting Row And Column Size

The size of the row and column are adjusted so that the text can best fit into the cell, you should not adjust the row and column until the row is filled with the text. To adjust the row or column, simply:

- place your cursor on the line that will cause the row or column to be adjusted.
- then wait till the cursor change to a **double-headed sword.**
- **double click and drag** to adjust the size of the row and column.

Education is the best legacy	Ball	Chair	Background	
	click and drag			
Agape	Divine			
The boy sit on the bench	construction		insolvent	

Watermarks

A watermark can be an image or text that is implanted across or horizontally over the paper to beautify and pass out more information, though the watermark is usually dim so that it will not cover the actual text on the paper. Add a watermark to your document with this simple trick.

- Tap on the **Design tab** and maneuver to the Page background section.
- Tap on the **watermark down arrow** and select a **watermark template** from the available list of watermarks that you can put across your document, you can as well edit and insert your text into those watermark templates.

Note: customize a watermark by selecting Custom watermark from the watermark drop-down menu, create your watermark within the Custom watermark dialog box either with graphic or text.

Remove the watermark by tapping the Remove watermark command from the watermark drop-down menu.

Cover Pages

A Cover Page is a front guide of every documentation, project, brochure, and other documents which gives a summarization of what your content entails.

How To Insert A Cover Page On Your Document

Go to "Insert tab"

At your left-hand side, you will see **"Cover Page"**

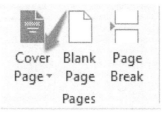

Click in to see multiple built-in "Cover Page" templates, select your preferred choice

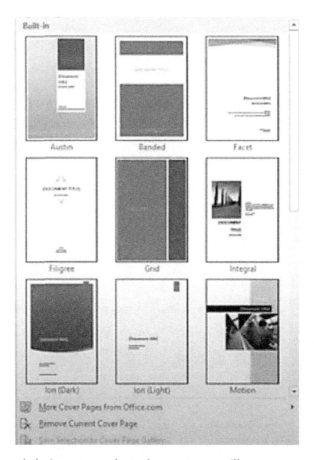

 Once you select your preferred choice, your selected cover page will occupy your front page

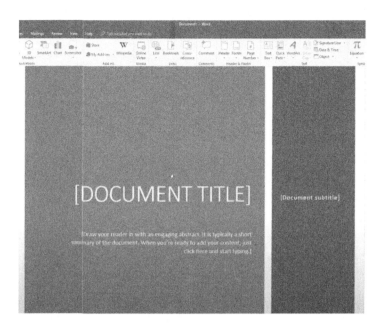

Then, you can start editing the title page, the writeup below your title, subtitle, and other aspects depending on the template you selected

Contents Pages

Microsoft Word includes a tool that lets you create a table of contents either automatically or manually using simple templates. You must write or prepare your document using the Word built-in headings in the Styles group to automatically insert a table of contents.

To Insert a Table of Contents:

- Ensure your document headings uses Word built-in headings styles
- Place your insertion point where you want the table of content to be.
- Go to the **References** ribbon.
- **Click** Table of Contents.
- A drop-down menu appears.
- Select an option:

The first two options automatically insert your table of contents with **all** your available headings.

The third option inserts the table of contents with placeholder texts and allows you to replace them with your own headings.

Select More Tables of Contents from Office.com **for more templates.**

Select the **Custom Table of Contents...** to customize your table. A dialog box appears, edit as desired, and press **OK**.

If you already have a table of content in your document, you can delete it by selecting **Remove Table of Contents.**

Updating Your Table Of Contents

Word does not update your table of content automatically if you make changes to your document. You will have to update it manually.

To update your Table of Content:

- Position your cursor in the table of content.
- Table borders appear with buttons at the top-left.

- Click the **Update Table** button.
- A dialog box appears.
- **Click the** Update entire table**.**
- Press **OK**.
- Word automatically updates your table.

Alternatively,

- Right-click on the table of content.
- A drop-down menu appears.
- Select **Update Field.** You can also select **Update Table** in the **Table of Contents** group in the **References** ribbon.
- A dialog box appears.
- **Click** Update the entire table**.**
- Click **OK**.

Note: Do not always forget to update your table after making significant changes that affect the headers or page numbers.

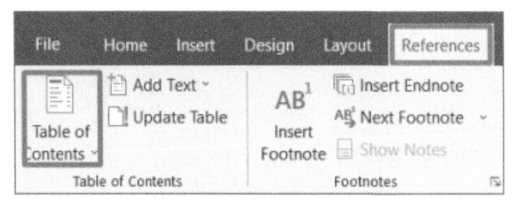

Indexes

With the **Index** group, you can add index in your document. Instead of doing this manually, the Index tab makes it fast and easy for you. With the **Mark Entry**, you mark the keywords you want to have in your index section, which is usually at the last pages of the document. To mark any keywords, just highlight the word, click the **Mark Entry** tool, and then click **Mark** button of the dialog box. And with **Insert Index** tool, you insert those keywords you have marked as entry.

Step by Step Guide on Inserting Index Automatically in Word

To insert index at the last page of your document, just follow this step-by-step guide:

- Highlight the words or phrases you want the have in your index
- Click **References** tab and then click **Mark Entry** tool to see a dialog box as shown below:

In the **Main entry,** the word inside is **Figure** because I highlighted the word before I clicked **Mark Entry** tool. Leave **Subentry** empty unless you have any to add there. Under **Options**, select **Current page** as shown in the image. Under **Page number format**, you can leave the boxes empty or tick any if you want the words or keywords to be written in bold or italic when they appear on the index page.

- Click **Mark** or **Mark All** button

When you click **Mark**, only where the word appears on the page at that moment will be recorded when you finally insert index page in your document. But if you click **Mark All,** where that word or keywords appear in the entire document will be recorded by Word 365 system.

- Click **Close** to close the dialog box

When you click the **Close** button, you will notice that all the paragraph marks and hidden symbols in your document will be shown. To return the document to its normal state, click the **Home** tab, and then click **Show/Hide Paragraph** tool which takes the shape "¶".

- Repeat step 1, 2, 3, 4 to add all the word, keywords, and phrases you want to have in the index page of the document
- Scroll down to one of the last pages of your document where you want to insert the index page and click at the spot.
- Click **References** tab and then click the **Insert Index** tool to show dialog box below:

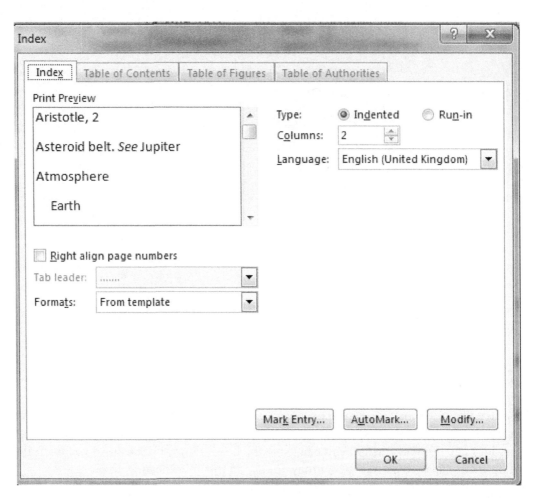

In the **Formats**, you can click the dropdown to choose the format you want. As you choose the format, you will see the sample of how the index will look like in the **Print Preview**.

- Click **Ok** button for the index to be inserted

Chapter 8: **Graphical Works in Microsoft Word**

Adding Images

A Picture is a static image used for different illustrations and purposes. Now, how do we insert pictures into our Word document?

- Go to "Insert" in your menu bar

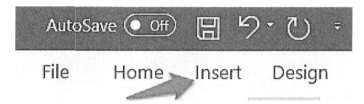

- Under the "Insert" tab, locate the "Illustrations" ribbon. In the "Illustrations" ribbon, select "Pictures"

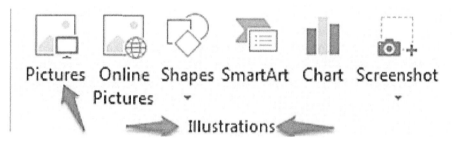

Once you click on "Pictures", a dialog box will pop up and direct you to your PC storage, locate the folder where your pictures are stored and click on your preferred image, then click "Insert"

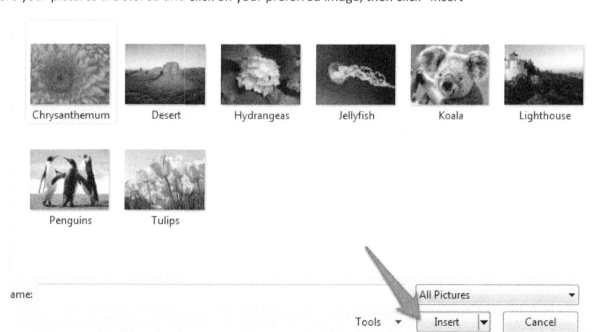

- Then, your image which is also the same as a picture will reflect on your Word document immediately. You can resize your image at the dots areas and rotate it if need be, using the curved arrow icon as illustrated below

Adding Clipart

Adding clip art and images to your document can be a great way to highlight important information or add a decorative accent to your existing text. You can import an image from your computer or browse the wide variety of Microsoft clip art to find the image you need. After inserting the image, you can format the text to fold the image.

- Choose the Insert tab to find clip art.
- In the Illustrations group, select Clip Art.
- In the Search for: section, enter keywords associated with the image you want to upload.
- Click the drop-down arrow in the Results column.
- Select the media types you do not want to view.
- Select the media type to display
- If you also want to search for clip art on **Office.com**, place a check mark next to Include **Office.com** Content. Otherwise, it will only search for clip art on your computer.
- Click Go.

To import clip art:

- Check the results of a clip art search.
- Insert the insertion point into the document where you want to insert the clip art.
- Click the image in the Clip Art window. It will appear in the document.
- Select Clip Art

You can also click the drop-down arrow next to an image in the Clip Art window to see more options.

Wrap Text Around Images

Word allows you to join texts and images together to explain a document. This is made possible by wrapping text around your image.

To wrap text around an image, follow the steps below:

Select the image you wish to wrap text around

Click on the **Format** menu that appears at top of the Word's ribbon and selects **Wrap text.**

Select any of the following in the **Warp Text** drop-down list

- **Square:** Choose this option if your image is square, and you wish to wrap the text around the square border of your image.
- **Top and Bottom:** Select this option if you want your image to stay on its own line, but between text on the top and button.
- **Tight:** Select this option if you wish to wrap text around a round or irregular-shaped image.
- **Through:** This option helps to customize the areas that the text will wrap. This is best used if you want to join the text with your image, and you do not wish to follow the line of your border.
- **Behind Text:** This option allows you to use the image as a watermark behind the text.
- **In Front of Text:** Select this option if you wish to display the image over the text. You can change the color, or make the text illegible.

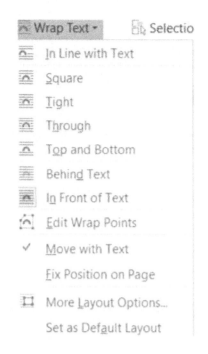

SmartArt

The **SmartArt** tool under **Insert** tab is used to communicate information virtually. It has graphical application. Through **SmartArt**, you will have access to many graphics integrated into Word 365 by Microsoft. SmartArt consists of many categories. The categories are **All, List, Process, Cycle, Hierarchy, Relationship, Matrix, Pyramid, Picture** and **Office.com**. Each of these categories contains graphics related to it. But **All** contains graphic designs that cut across the other categories.

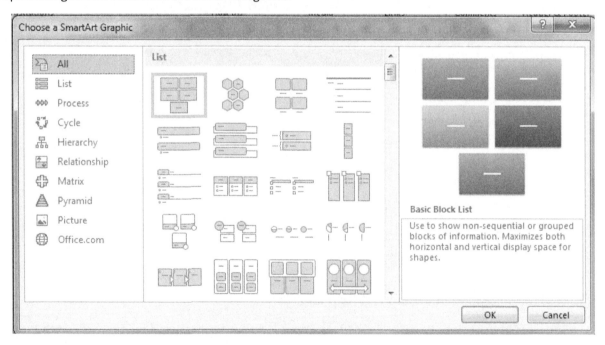

In this section, I will walk you through on how to use SmartArt tool.

Step by Step Guide on how to use SmartArt Tool

To apply SmartArt tool in Word 365, take the following steps:

- Click your Word 365 to open and then select **Blank document** to open the Word environment
- Click **Insert** tab and select **SmartArt** which is in **Illustrations** category
- Select any graphic representation from the graphics category

You can choose from any category depending on what you are preparing. Take for instance I want to have graphical representation of salespersons positions in the company I work, I will choose one illustration under **Pyramid** category.

- Click **Ok** button

Once you click the **Ok** button at the right-hand side of the graphics gallery, the graphics will be inserted into your Word 365 environment.

- Start designing your graphics to fit into what you want to build at the end.

Since in this illustration I am building with pyramid to show the ranks of salespersons in insurance, I have to start my design. There is provision where I am to type texts and they reflect in the main pyramid stage. If I want to add more pyramid steps, I will right-click in any of the stage and select to **Add shape** option. From there I can choose to add the shape before or after. You can also adjust the position of the design by press and drag with your cursor.

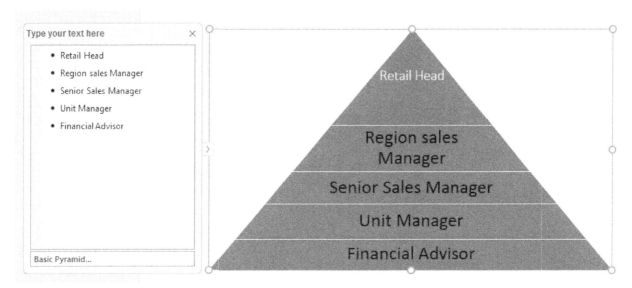

Click out of the section after design

Chapter 9: **Tables and Charts**

Adding Tables

Creating a table has been for different purposes such as for grading, calculating, listing of names, items, and so on. To create a table, simply follow this procedure

Go to the "Insert" tab

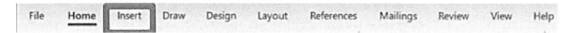

Below the "Insert tab", you will see "Table", click the little arrow under to get the dropdown table options

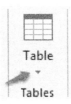

Once you click on the arrow, you get the dropdown rows and columns which is known as "Table Grid". Select the numbers of rows and columns you want, then, click on the last selection of row and column to display it on your Word document

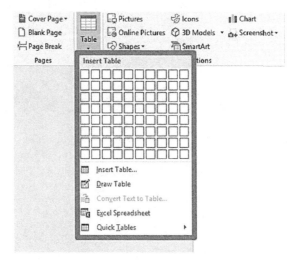

Assuming we pick five rows and two columns, at the last selection, right-click on your mouse to effect it on your Word document

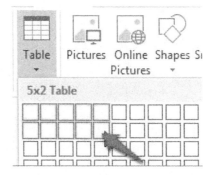

Here is the result that you will have on your Word document

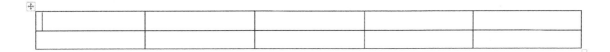

Quick Table

Quick tables are tables you can modify for your use. To begin, Put your cursor where you want to Insert the table. Click on the Insert tab on the Ribbon. Select table in the table group followed by quick table from the drop-down menu as shown in figure 3. Choose the table you want from the gallery. Then enter your content by typing over or deleting the table example text.

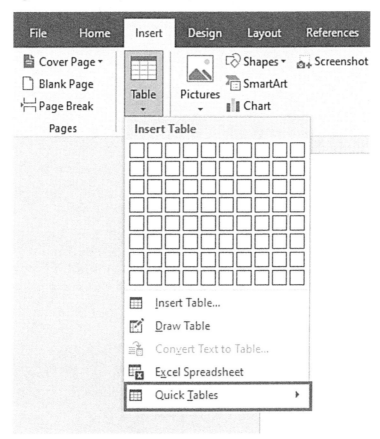

How Do I Enter Text into a Table

Once you have selected the number of rows (horizontal) and columns (vertical), then your table will be displayed in your Word document. Assuming it is three rows and five columns, place your mouse cursor on the table to type your text and number

Then, start typing your words inside

Number	Text	
1	One	
2	Two	
3	Three	
4	Four	

Table Styles

Go to "Insert"

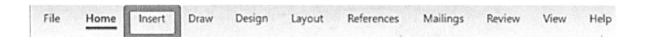

Below the "Insert tab" you will see "Table", click the little arrow to get the dropdown table options

Once you click on the arrow, you get the dropdown rows and columns which is known as "Table Grid". Select the numbers of rows and columns, then click on the last selection of row and column to display it on your Word document

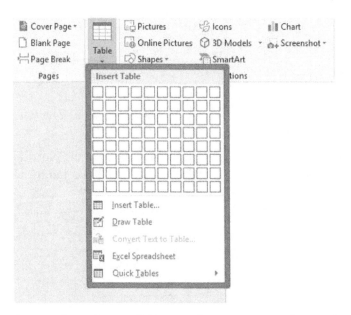

Once you have selected the number of rows (horizontal) and columns (vertical), then your table will be displayed in your Word document, let's assume it is four rows and three columns

Click inside one of the columns, once you do this, it becomes active to receive text

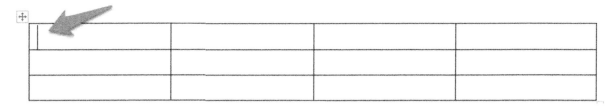

Immediately, the menu bar will show "Table Tools" which are the "Design" table tab and "Layout" table tab, click on "Design table tab"

Design   Layout

Under "Design", you will see "table" styles which consist of predefined table styles to use, click on any colorful style to see its effect on your table

Table Styles

You can also click on the dropdown arrow on your right-hand side to view other table options

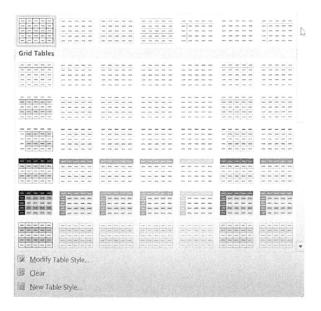

Once selected, your created table will be transformed into the predefined template

Note: "Table Tools" only show up whenever the table cell is active.

Table Tools

Formatting Tables

Borders are the lines that form table edges. With borders, you can decorate your table and design it to your preferred choice. How to decorate your table with borders and colors will be explained step by step below

- To save time because of the process of creating another table, we will be using our calendar table. Highlight your heading cell which is "January 2022" or you point your cursor into the "January 2022" row. Note you can use any cell, just for a well-ordered work, we will use the heading cell (January 2022)

January 2022						
Sunday	Monday	Tuesday	Wednesday	Thursday	Friday	Saturday
						1
2	3	4	5	6	7	8
9	10	11	12	13	14	15
16	17	18	19	20	21	22
23	24	25	26	27	28	29
30	31					

Then, the table options will appear named "Table tools", under it is "Design" and "Layout", click on "Layout"

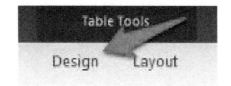

- At your right-hand side, locate "Borders"

Click on "Borders" to select a different line style format to replace the default borders. For example, we could choose a triple line border

We can also change the line weight to one and a half point (1$\frac{1}{2}$ pt)

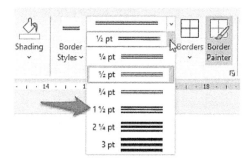

We can also change the border color by picking the orange color

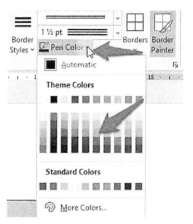

Once your color has been selected, the "Border Styles", "Line Weight", "Line Styles" and "Pen Color" will have the effect of your chosen color. Note that your "Border Painter" is selected automatically

Once your "Border Painter" is selected, your mouse cursor will change to pen cursor, simply place it on the line edge you want your triple line and color to affect. Note, if you place it wrongly, you will need to select "Border Painter" again

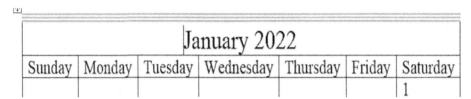

January 2022						
Sunday	Monday	Tuesday	Wednesday	Thursday	Friday	Saturday
						1

But there is also another way out without having to click and wrongly place line edges; simply click on "Borders"

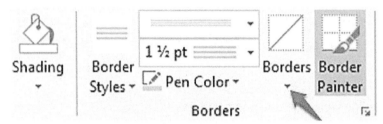

Then, select what area you want your border to cover such as "Bottom Border", "Top Border", "Left Border", "Right Border" and so on. We will be clicking on "All Borders"

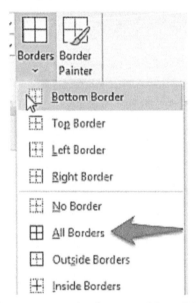

Once "All Borders" has been selected, your created calendar table will be formatted on your active cell which is "January 2022" where your mouse cursor is pointing.

January 2022						
Sunday	Monday	Tuesday	Wednesday	Thursday	Friday	Saturday
						1
2	3	4	5	6	7	8

NOTE: If you want the remaining rows and columns to also be formatted, then, you need to highlight the entire table to perform such an operation.

You can also add shade color on the background of "January 2022" by changing the white background. To do this, click on "Shading"

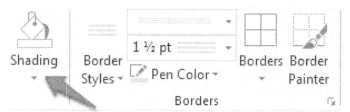

Select your preferred color. For illustration, I will pick the gray color to achieve a color blend.

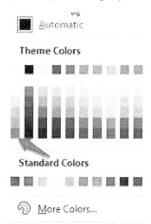

Your outcome if you choose the same color with me, will be the illustration below

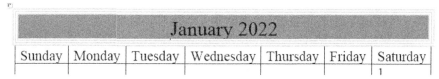

Exploring more on Borders

In continuation of *"Decorating your table with borders and colors"*. It is important to note that there is also more to Border Style

Still on our created calendar table illustration

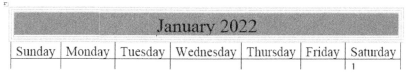

- Click on "Design" table tools

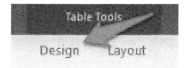

At your left-hand side, you will see a dropdown arrow, click on it

You will be brought here, where all our formatted styles are reviewed and edited. It consists of "Borders settings", "Page Border settings" and "Shading settings". If you remember, previously, we choose an orange color, that is why you are seeing orange color and one and half width. Click on the "Shading" option

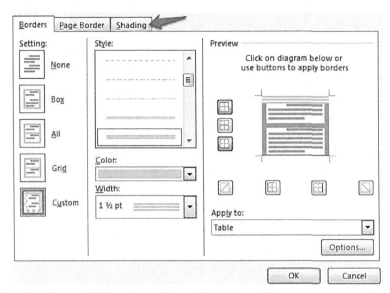

Once you click on "Shading", you will be brought to this page, where you can set your "Shading Patterns", "Style", "Color" and "Apply to". Under "Apply to", select "Table", then click "Ok" to see the effect

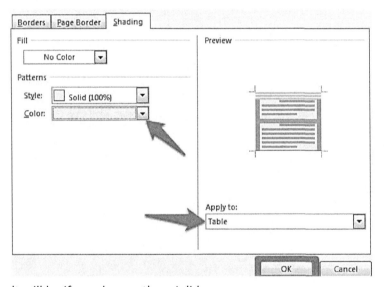

Here is what your result will be if you do exactly as I did

January 2022						
Sunday	Monday	Tuesday	Wednesday	Thursday	Friday	Saturday
						1
2	3	4	5	6	7	8
9	10	11	12	13	14	15
16	17	18	19	20	21	22
23	24	25	26	27	28	29
30	31					

Adding Row and Column

Once you select the number of rows and columns and you have inputted your texts, there is a possibility of needing an additional table to continue your content, simply place your cursor at the edge of your table as illustrated below.

Position	Type	Location
Computer Engineer	Full-time, two months	Clearwater
Software Developer	Full-time, open-ended	Tampa
UI Designer	Part-time, two months	St. Petersburg

Once you see the plus sign (+), click on it, another empty single row and column will be created

Position	Type	Location
Computer Engineer	Full-time, two months	Clearwater
Software Developer	Full-time, open-ended	Tampa
UI Designer	Part-time, two months	St. Petersburg

You can then fill up the empty rows and columns with your desired text

Position	Type	Location
Computer Engineer	Full-time, two months	Clearwater
Project Assistant	Full-time, three months	Coral Springs
Software Developer	Full-time, open-ended	Tampa
UI Designer	Part-time, two months	St. Petersburg

Resizing Rows o Columns

Place your cursor on any column, click on the layout tab and click on cell size group there is a height option, click to expand it and the height of the column increases, same with weight, etc.

To Get an equal height of each column, click on distribute rows and all rows will have equal height. Same with the column, click on distribute column to get an equal column.

To resize an entire table, click the resizing handle in the bottom right of the table. You may be required to move your pointer over the table to reveal the handle. Then drag the table to the size you want upon the + sign on the bottom side of the table.

Merge Cells

Beyond explanation, it is also important to understand the little element that the big element is made up of. "Cell" is the inputted part where your text and number are inserted into. So, why merge cells? Merging of cells is mostly needed for various reasons such as naming your table, constructing a calendar.

The month and year (for example, January 2022) need to occupy the first rows in a bold and large format to give a clear update on what the table is all about as seen in the image below

January 2022						
Sunday	Monday	Tuesday	Wednesday	Thursday	Friday	Saturday
						1
2	3	4	5	6	7	8
9	10	11	12	13	14	15
16	17	18	19	20	21	22
23	24	25	26	27	28	29
30	31					

Then, how do we merge cells?

Since I have shown you how to insert tables, Let's assume we want to create something similar to the calendar format above. For us to merge our table, if you count the rows, you will notice it is seven (7) in number, while the columns are eight (8) in number including the heading (January 2022). This is also an opportunity to create a calendar with Office Word document. After creating your table, input the text and number in its various location

January 2022						
Sunday	Monday	Tuesday	Wednesday	Thursday	Friday	Saturday
						1
2	3	4	5	6	7	8
9	10	11	12	13	14	15
16	17	18	19	20	21	22
23	24	25	26	27	28	29
30	31					

Then, place your cursor at the beginning of "January 2022"

January 2022						
Sunday	Monday	Tuesday	Wednesday	Thursday	Friday	Saturday
						1
2	3	4	5	6	7	8
9	10	11	12	13	14	15
16	17	18	19	20	21	22
23	24	25	26	27	28	29
30	31					

Once your cursor is blinking at the beginning of January 2022, simply hold down "Shift key" on your keyboard with the "forward Arrow" at the right-hand side of your keyboard. It will be highlighting your first row, once your highlighting gets to the last row, release your hand from the "Shift & "Arrow keys" on your keyboard, below is where the highlighting of your rows should stop

January 2022						
Sunday	Monday	Tuesday	Wednesday	Thursday	Friday	Saturday
						1
2	3	4	5	6	7	8
9	10	11	12	13	14	15
16	17	18	19	20	21	22
23	24	25	26	27	28	29
30	31					

After highlighting it, go to the "menu bar", click on "Layout"

Under "Layout" look at your left-hand side, you will see the "Merge" ribbon, click on "Merge cells"

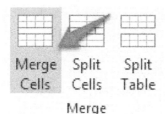

By default, your highlighted row will be merged as one, you will also notice the column lines that separate the entire table is no longer applicable to the "January 2022" row

January 2022						
Sunday	Monday	Tuesday	Wednesday	Thursday	Friday	Saturday
						1
2	3	4	5	6	7	8
9	10	11	12	13	14	15
16	17	18	19	20	21	22
23	24	25	26	27	28	29
30	31					

Align Cell Text

Simply go to "Insert tab"

Below "Insert", you will see "Table", click the little arrow to get the dropdown options

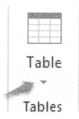

Once you click on "Table", you get the "Table Grid", select the numbers of rows and columns you want to work with, then click on the last selection of rows and column to display it on your Word document

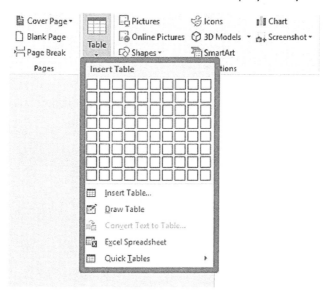

Once it appears on your Word document, you can type your text into it. For us to see how to align a table, I will use my previous table to illustrate how to align your table

Position	Type	Location
Computer Engineer	Full-time, two months	Clearwater
Project Assistant	Full-time, three months	Coral Springs
Software Developer	Full-time, open-ended	Tampa
UI Designer	Part-time, two months	St. Petersburg

Once you click any part of your table a little plus (+) sign will appear on your left-hand side, click on it

Position	Type	Location
Computer Engineer	Full-time, two months	Clearwater
Project Assistant	Full-time, three months	Coral Springs
Software Developer	Full-time, open-ended	Tampa
UI Designer	Part-time, two months	St. Petersburg

All your table will be automatically highlighted

Position	Type	Location
Computer Engineer	Full-time, two months	Clearwater
Project Assistant	Full-time, three months	Coral Springs
Software Developer	Full-time, open-ended	Tampa
UI Designer	Part-time, two months	St. Petersburg

Then, go to your "home" tab

 By your right-hand side under the "Paragraph" ribbon, there are four types of alignment; left alignment, center alignment, right alignment, and justify alignment. For understanding, we will be using center alignment to see the effect, because by default your table is on left alignment; simply click the "**center alignment**" which is the second alignment icon from your left

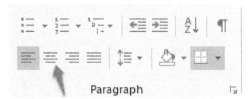

Paragraph

You can press the shortcut, "Ctrl + E" on your keyboard, your table will be moved to the center point. Once you select center alignment as illustrated, here's what it will look like

For further information about any of these new jobs, or a complete listing of jobs that are available through the Career Center, please call Mary Walker-Huelsman at (727) 555-0030 or visit our website at www.fpcc.pro/careers.

Position	Type	Location
Computer Engineer	Full-time, two months	Clearwater
Project Assistant	Full-time, three months	Coral Springs
Software Developer	Full-time, open-ended	Tampa
UI Designer	Part-time, two months	St. Petersburg

To help prepare yourself before applying for these jobs, we recommend that you review the following articles on our website at www.fpcc.pro/careers.

Text Direction

Create a table of your choice as you were taught earlier, you can decide to replicate the one I'm using for illustration, two (2) rows, and three (3) columns. Make sure your cursor is blinking inside the one cell

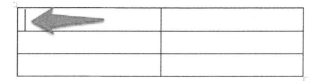

Next, look above and locate "Table tools". Under "Table Tools", click on "Layout"

Then, locate "Properties" and click on it

Once you click on "Properties", a dialog box will be opened titled "Table" properties, under "Table", locate "Text wrapping", by default it is on "None", simply select "Around" and then press "Ok"

Adding a Chart

How to Insert "Chart"

Select "Chart" in the "Illustrations" ribbon

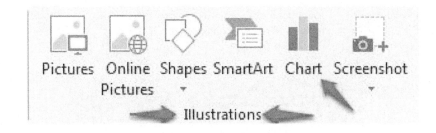

A dialog box will appear consisting of the "All Charts" features such as "Column", "Line", "Pie", "Bar", "Area", and other charts. It's majorly used to view the estimation of data after it has been concluded.

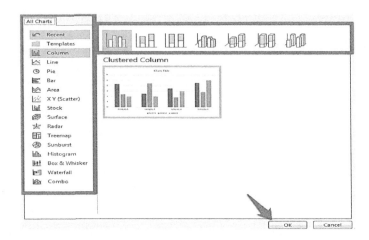

Chapter 10: Templates

Finding a Template

MS word document can be created either from a blank document or from the various available template that is available on the MS word 2022 start screen, after the creation of the document you can store such document on your PC or the iCloud. Study the below steps to get acquainted with the document creation:

- Tap on the **File tab** and choose **New from File backstage** on the left side of the screen.
- Select a **blank new document thumbnail** to create a blank new document or select the **desired template** from the available offline template or search for the various templates on the internet.

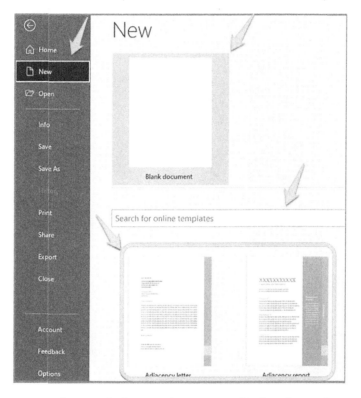

Note: you can create a document with a quick shortcut by pressing (Ctrl + N), word permit you to create as many documents as you want, each document can have several pages.

Making Your Own Template

Follow the steps below to create a new template;

- Click on the Ctrl + N button to create a new document.
- Locate the File tab and choose the Save As option.
- Click on the Browse option.
- Open the Save As option and choose Word Template.
- Insert a name that can be used to describe the template and click the Save button.

Create Document from Saved Template

MS word document can be created either from a blank document or from the various available template that is available on MS word 365 start screen, after the creation of the document you can store such document to your PC or the iCloud. Study the below steps to get acquainted with the document creation:

- Tap on the **File tab** and choose **New from File backstage** at the left side of the screen.

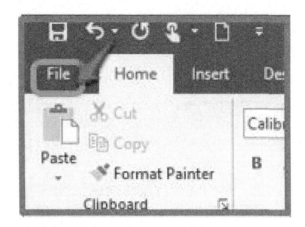

- Select a **blank new document thumbnail** to create a blank new document or select the **desired template** from the available offline template or search for the various templates on the internet.

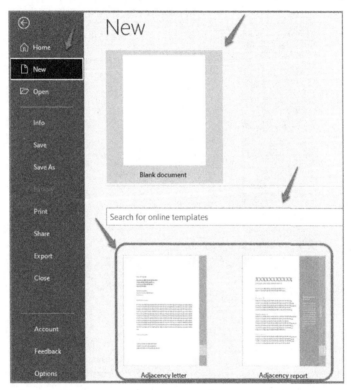

Note: you can create a document with a quick shortcut by pressing (Ctrl + N), word permit you to create as many documents as you want, each document can have several pages.

Chapter 11: **Mailing**

Printing on Envelopes

- Go to "Mailings"

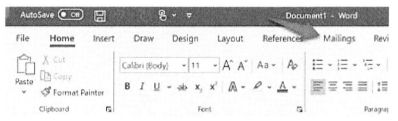

- Under the "Mailings" tab, at your left-hand side, you will see "Envelopes", click on it

- Simply fill in all the required details such as "Delivery address", "Return address", "Add to document" if need be. Once everything has been verified, click on "Print"

Mail Merge

Mail Merge is a nice property that Microsoft integrated into her Word 365 software. With the mail merge tool, you can send mail to large number of people once. Just arrange their email addresses and the other details the way they are to be and send the mail once to them.

Take these steps to start and finish mail merge:

- In your current document, type the mail you want to send the way you want it to appear to the recipients.
- Click the **Mailings** tab followed by **Start Mail Merge** command
- From the options, select how you want the mail communicated to your recipients (preferably **Normal Word Document** since the mail is composed using that channel).

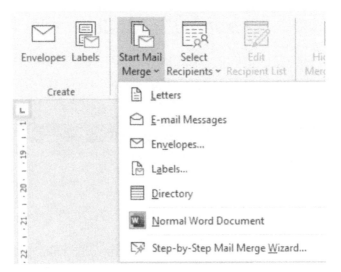

- Click Select Recipients command

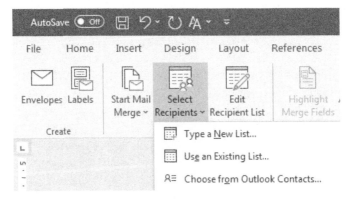

- As you are shown some channels where you can get the list of the people you want to send mail to, you can select any. If for example you have prepared their names, phone numbers, email addresses, home addresses and other details in an excel spreadsheet which is saved in a folder of your computer, just select **Use an Existing List** and upload the file from your computer. But here I assume you have not done that so select the option **Type a New List** which will display a dialog box that I show below:

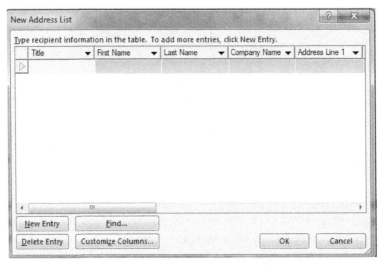

- In the dialog box, click under each heading and fill the required information. Fill the necessary information and when you are done click **Ok** button. Know that you must not fill all the information in the table, but first name, last name, company name, city, state, zip code, country, and address are very important for you to get the expected result. Also, when you are done with filling a recipient's detail, click **New Entry** button to start filling a new one. Do this until you fill the details of the number of recipients you want to have.

- Click the beginning of your document where in a normal letter standard the address of the recipient is positioned and click **Address Block** command and in the dialog box that will show up click **Ok** command.
- Click **Greeting Line** command, in the dialog box, Select any option in the Greeting line format and an option for the invalid recipient names.

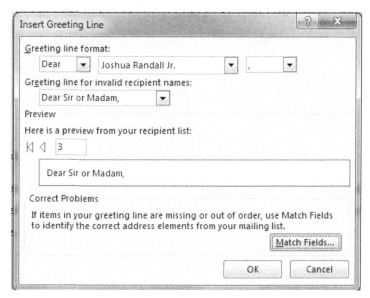

- Click **OK** button to save your selection.
- Click the **Insert Merge Field** command and choose the suitable option which is usually **Name**.
- Click **Preview Results** command to be shown how your mail merge will look like when sent or printed out.

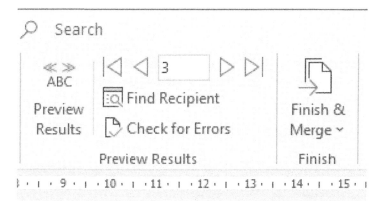

Click the arrow to see how each recipient's detail will appear as the mail is sent out.

- Click **Finish and Merge** and select **Print Documents** or **Send Email Messages** option and fill in the expected data.

Chapter 12: **Check your Spelling & Grammar**

Checking Spelling Errors

You can check for spelling errors in your documents by either correcting spelling errors one at a time or running a spelling check.

Correcting Spelling Errors One Step at a Time

You can correct your spelling errors without running the spell check method.

To do this:

- Locate the word that is underlined with a red line and then right-click on it
- Select the correct spelling from the **Spelling** shortcut menu
- After doing this, the word misspelled is replaced with the word you right-clicked on

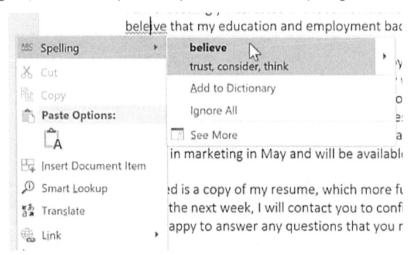

Running the Spell Check

Correcting spelling errors one by one can be a waste of time; therefore, you use the Spell check which is faster. To start your spell check, you can use any of the following methods

- Press **F7**
- Go to the **Status bar** and click on the **Proofing Error** button

- Go to the Review tab and click on **Spelling & Grammar**

- The Editor task pane displays where you can view the number of spellings and grammar errors in your documents.
- Click on Spelling in the task pane to see the suggestions provided for a misspelling, and then click on the correct spelling.

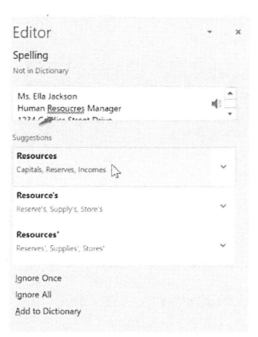

Preventing Text from Being Spell Checked

There are certain words in your documents that cannot be spell-checked especially words like address lists, lines of computer codes, and foreign languages such as French, Spanish, etc. To prevent text of this kind from being spell-checked, follow the steps below

- Select the text.
- On the **Review tab**, click on the **Language** button, and select **Set Proofing Language.**

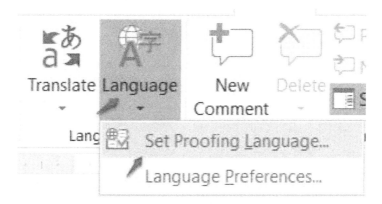

- In the **Language** dialog box, click on the **Do not check spelling or grammar** check box

Correcting Grammatical Errors

Just like how spellings are corrected, the same techniques apply to correcting grammatical errors.

Correcting Grammatical Errors One Step at a Time

You can correct grammar errors by following the steps below

- Locate the word that is underlined with a blue line and right-click on it
- Correct the grammatical error from the **Grammar** shortcut menu
- After doing this, the grammatical error will be replaced with the word you right-clicked on.

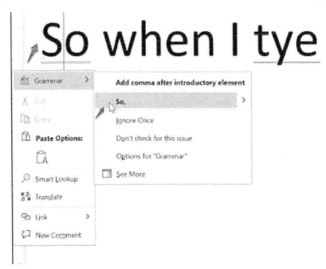

Correcting Grammatical Errors Using Editor Task Pane

You can use the Editor task pane to correct your grammatical errors. Primarily, you will need to open the Editor task pane. To open the Editor task pane, you any of the following methods

- Press **F7**
- Go to the **Status bar** and click on the **Proofing Error** button

- Go to the Review tab and click on **Spelling & Grammar**

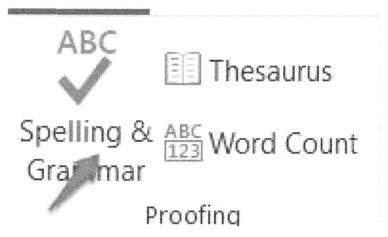

- When the **Editor** task pane opens, select **Grammar** in the task pane and then click on the option under **Suggestions.**

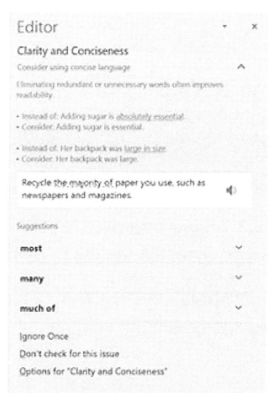

Ignoring Errors

It is no doubt that the spelling and grammar check is aimed at correcting errors, yet, it is not always correct. There are several instances where Word will see some words as errors when they are not. This happens a lot when the names and other proper nouns are not included in the dictionary, especially in foreign languages, or computer codes.

However, you can choose to ignore any word that is tagged to be an error by Word from the options provided by Word for both spelling and grammar checks.

For Spelling errors, you can choose any of the following options

- **Ignore:** This skips the misspelled word without changing it but stops on it if the same word appears again.
- **Ignore All:** This skips the misspelled word without changing it, and it also skips the same word if it appears again.
- **Add to Dictionary:** This adds the word to the dictionary so that it will not come up as an error. Ensure that the words are correctly spelled before adding them to the dictionary.

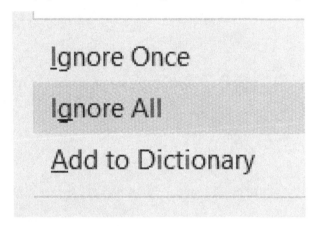

For Grammar errors, you get to choose just one option:

- **Ignore Once**: This skips the word or phrase without changing it.

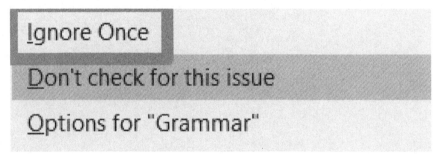

Customizing Spelling & Grammar Check

By default, there are some errors your proofing tools ignore without correcting, which you will want your proofing tools to correct.

To include all these in your spelling and grammar check, follow the steps given below

- Go to the **Backstage view** by clicking on the **File** menu.

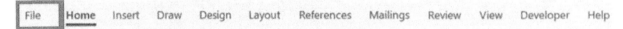

- Click on **Options** on the left pane.

- In the **Word Options** dialog box, click on **Proofing.**

- **On the left-hand side** when correcting spelling and grammar in Word**, click on** Settings.

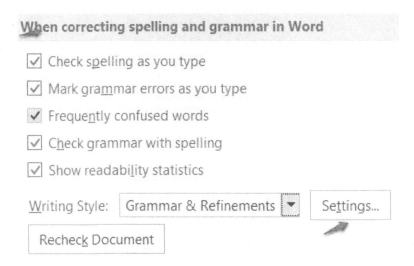

- In the **Grammar Settings** dialog box, select the options you wish to add to your spellings and grammar check, and then click on **Ok.**

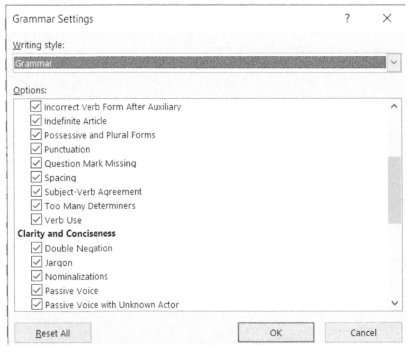

Hiding Spellings and Grammar Errors in a Document

In case you want to share your document with a person, and you do not want the person to see the red and blue lines. All you need to do is turn off the automatic spelling and grammar checks. Not only will the errors be hidden on your computer, but they also will not be displayed when viewed on another computer. To hide the spelling and grammar errors, follow the steps given below

- Go to the **Backstage view** by clicking on the **File** menu
- Click on **Options** on the left pane
- In the **Word Options** dialog box, click on **Proofing**

Go to Exceptions **and click on the checkboxes;** Hide spelling errors in this document only **and** Hide grammar in this document only.

Editing your Custom Dictionary

Word permits you to create a correctly spelled word that MS word has labeled as a misspelled word, as soon as you add them to a custom dictionary such texts will be recognized as correct spelling. U can add a word to the custom dictionary and remove any text. To do so, simply:

- Tap the **File tab and select the Option** from the file backstage to open the Word Options dialog box.
- Select **proofing** from the box and click the **custom dictionary.**

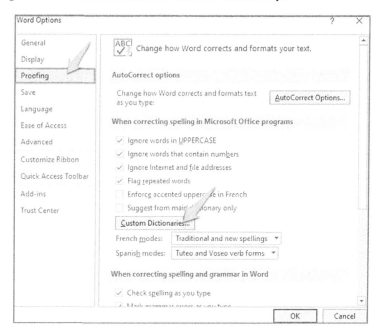

- The custom Dictionary dialog box will come forth, select the **"Custom. (Dic (Default)"** you may not have any other option apart from "Custom. Dic (Default)" unless you upgrade your PC.
- Then tap **Edit word list**, and a dialog box will be opened, which will provide you with a box where you can **add a new word to the Custom dictionary**, and also you will see the previous list of the word you have added, to erase any word from the list, kindly click on any word and choose **delete.**

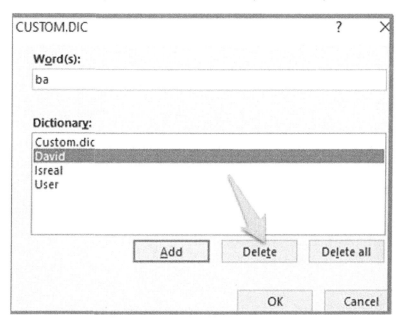

Thesaurus

The Thesaurus is a software tool in a Microsoft Word document that allows you to look for synonyms and antonyms of selected words.

There are three ways to open and use the Thesaurus:

- Press Shift + F7
- Right-click on any word, select **Synonyms** and then click on **Thesaurus**

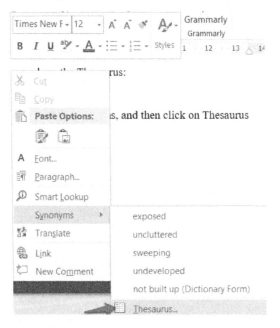

- Go to the **Review** tab, and click on the **Thesaurus** button

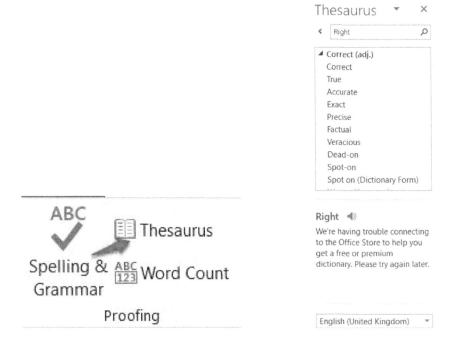

Rewrite Suggestions

Another newly added feature of Microsoft Word 365 is the "Rewrite Suggestions" which gives subscribers access to rephrase words. Let's see how it works

Assuming I typed the below sentence

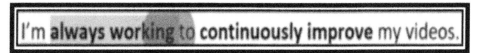

Now, you highlight the area which you want to rephrase. Let's assume it is "always working" in the above illustration

Right-click on the selected text, a dialog box will appear, locate and click on "Rewrite Suggestions"

Once you click on "Rewrite Suggestions", another dialog box will appear at your right-hand side with a suggestion of my highlighted text instead of "always working to" you can say "constantly working to" or "working all the time to"; I will click on "constantly working to"

Then my highlighted text will be replaced with "constantly working to".

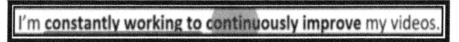

Search & Replace

This allows you to use the Navigation pane to search for specific words or phrases in a document. To use this command, follow the steps given below

127

- Go to the **Home** tab, click on **Find** and the **Navigation pane** appears.

- In the **Search document** box in the **Navigation pane**, enter the text you wish to find.
- Use the arrows under the search box to move to **Previous** or **Next** search results.
- When you are done, click on the **X** button to close the **Navigation pane**

Advanced Find Command

This command allows you to search your documents for more specific items, such as match cases, wildcards, whole words, etc.

To use the Advanced Find command, follow the steps given below

- Go to the **Home** tab, click on the **Find** button list arrow and select **Advanced Find**

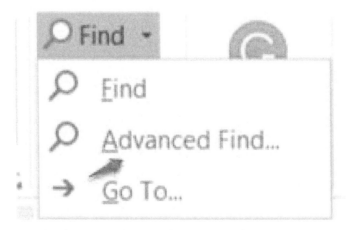

- In the **Find and Replace** dialog box opens, enter the word of the **Find** box.

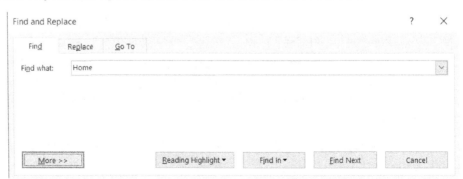

- Click on the **More** button; the More button allows you to set some options such as Match Case, Wildcards, Match prefix, etc. on how to search.

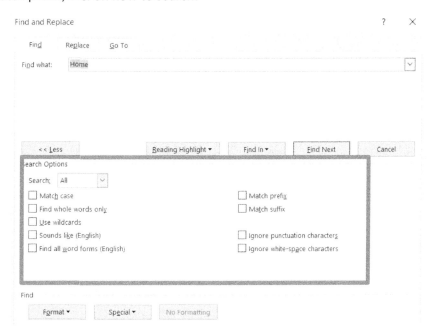

- Click on **Find Next** and Word searches from the current cursor location to the end of the document. If you click on **Find All**, Word searches the entire document.
- Then click on **Close** at the top of the dialog box.

The Replace Command

The Replace command allows you to find any word in your document and replace it with another. This can come in handy when you have misspelled a word in many places and wish to correct it. To use the Replace command, follow the steps given below

Go to the **Home** tab, click on **Replace**

In the **Find and Replace** dialog box, open the **Replace t**ab

Enter the word you need to find in the **Find what** text field

Enter the word you want to replace within the **Replace with** text field

Select any of the replacement options.

- **Replace**: This replaces individual instances of the text.

- **Replace All**: This replaces every instance of the text in the entire document.

Click on **Ok**

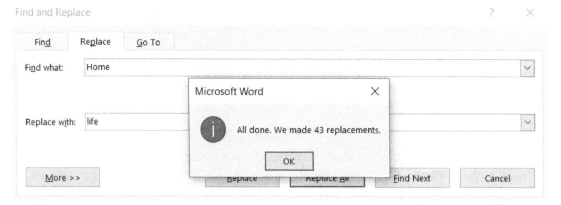

Then Press **Close** when you are done

Chapter 13: **Office Add-ins**

Word 365 is a great computer application, which has a lot to write on. So, the learning is on how to complete other possible tasks which are possible through any tool available in **Insert** button of Word 365.

The Components of Add-ins Category

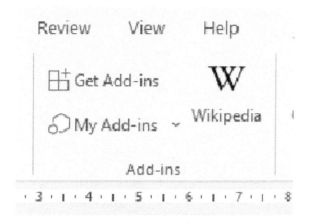

As shown in the picture above, the components of **Add-ins** category are **Get Add-ins**, **My Add-ins** and **Wikipedia**. As the component names sound, so is their roles. I will explain further.

Working with Add-ins Category

Just like any other tool used in Word 365, **Add-ins** tool is one of them. The **Add-ins** can be found when you click **Insert** menu. When you enable **Add-ins** in Word 365, it adds custom commands and new features to Office programs. This makes you to work more productively in the Word application. With Add-ins security settings feature, you can deny hackers access to your important Word files. Add-ins can be purchased from its developers online and they get installed in your Word 365. But before you install any add-ins in your Word 365, make sure you trust the source.

Get Add-ins

When you click **Get Add-ins,** a new word window shows some add-ins you can purchase or get for free from the Office store. The screenshot is shown below:

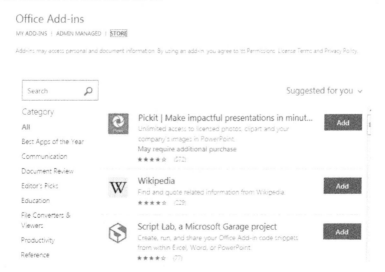

Make sure your computer is connected to internet before you click **Get Add-ins.** If you have any add-in in mind before clicking the **Get Add-ins** button, you can search for it using the search box on the top part of the interface. Click **Add** button, grant permission to install the add-in in your Word 365, and then start using it after the installation.

My Add-ins

Through **My Add-ins** button, you can see the add-ins you have already installed in your Word 365. By default, if you click that button, it will notify you that you have no add-ins installed in your Word app. But if you have installed any in your Word app and click on it, it will show you the available one. You can also delete already installed add-in which you do not want to have again through this tool.

Printed in Great Britain
by Amazon

29274012R00077